MANDALA FUN
Adult Coloring Book
Volume 2

By Cheryl Colors
#cherylcolors

www.adultcoloringworldwide.com
https://globaldoodlegems.wordpress.com

Copyright © 2016 Cheryl Colors
All rights reserved.
Published by Global Doodle Gems and Adult Coloring Worldwide.
ISBN-13: 978-8793449107 / ISBN-10: 8793449100

Cover page, editing and formatting by #anniecolors

··· DEDICATION ···

This page is dedicated to all the colorists around the world who have contributed their colourful pages to our community no matter if you're a beginner or advanced.

You've helped adult colouring grow into a hobby that we can all share and enjoy with everyone.

LET'S GET COLORING!!

• USE THIS PAGE TO TEST YOUR COLORS •

Tip: Placing an extra sheet of paper underneath your coloring pages can help to prevent bleed-through when coloring.

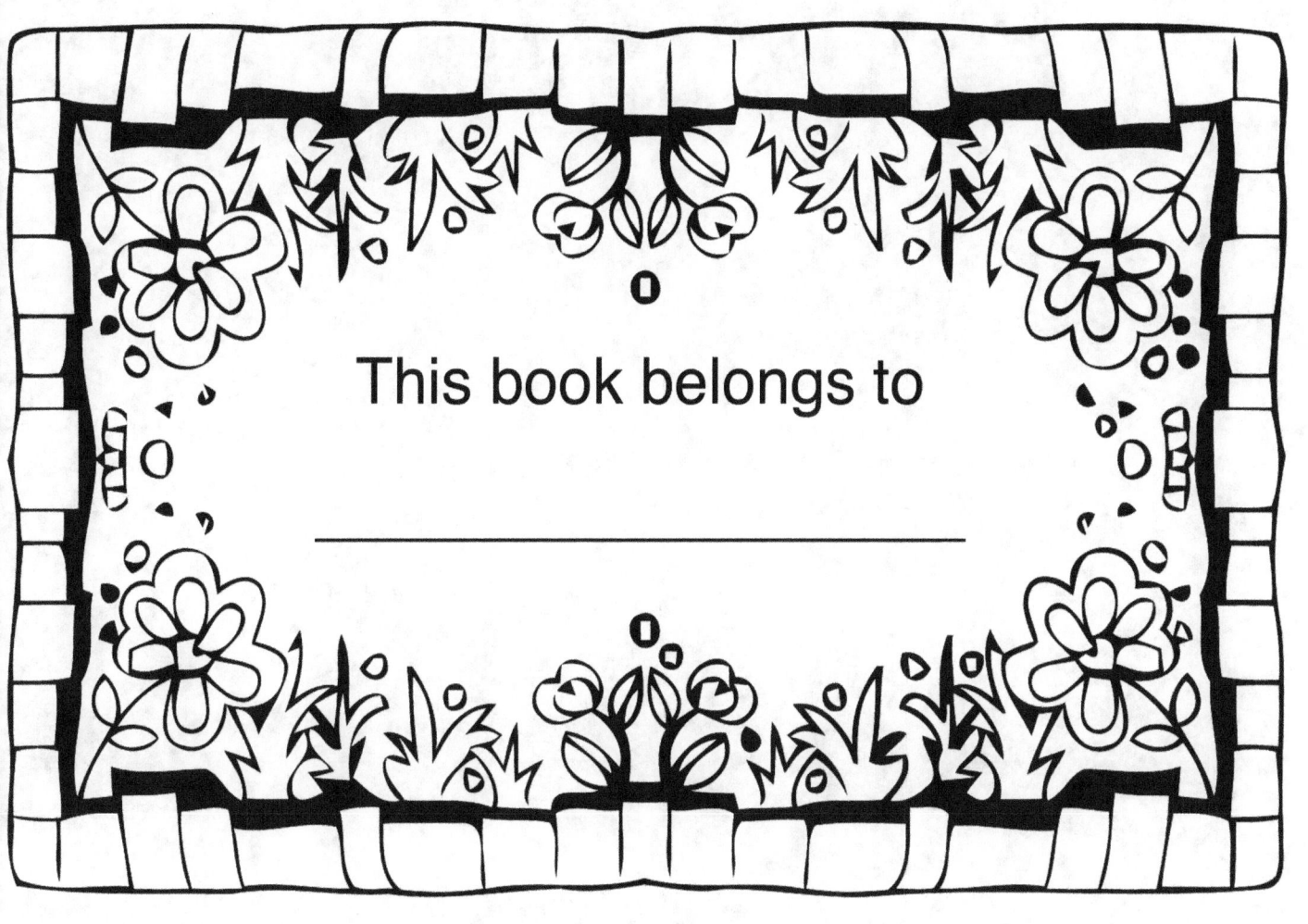

MANDALA FUN
Adult Coloring Book Volume 2

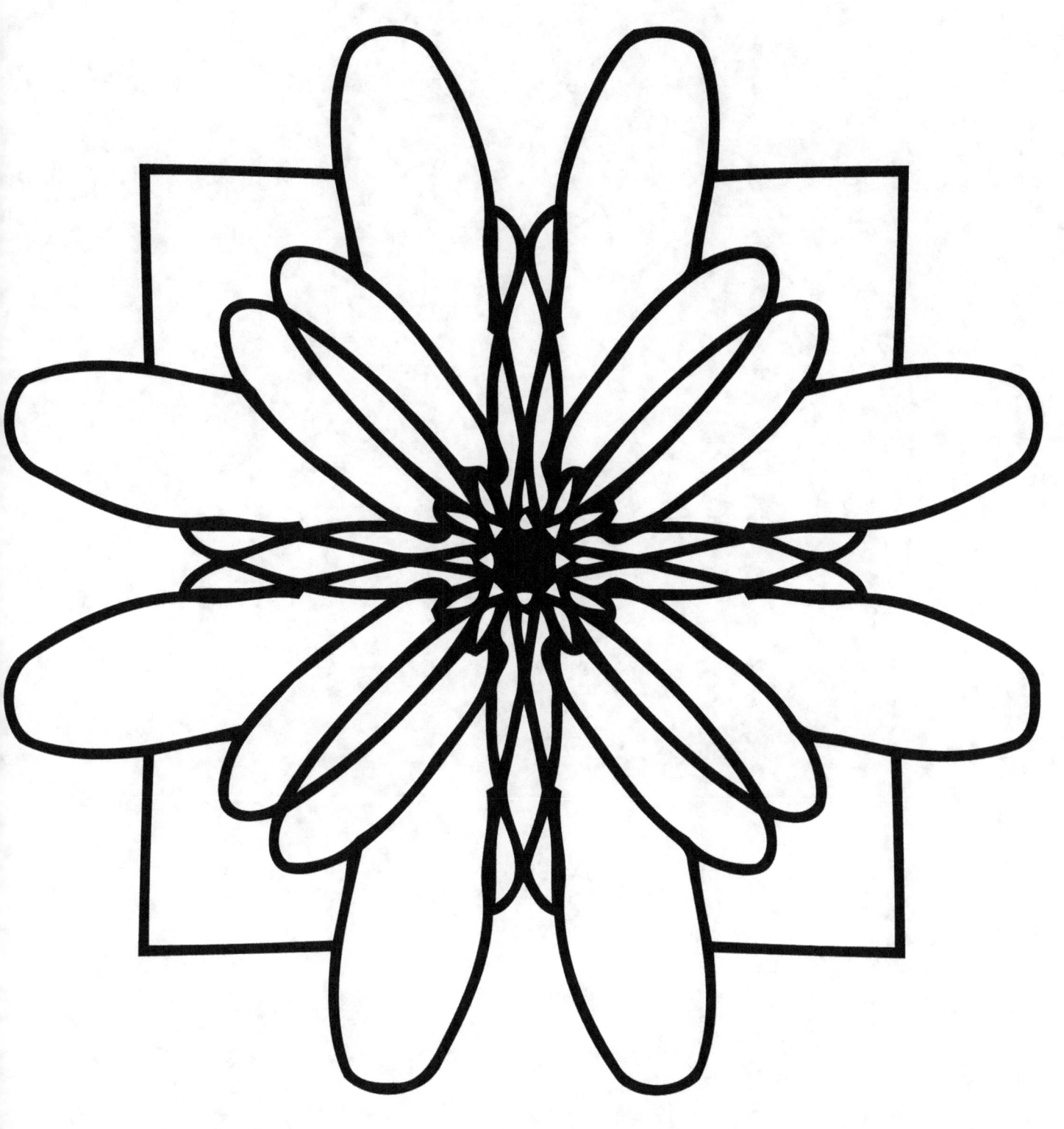

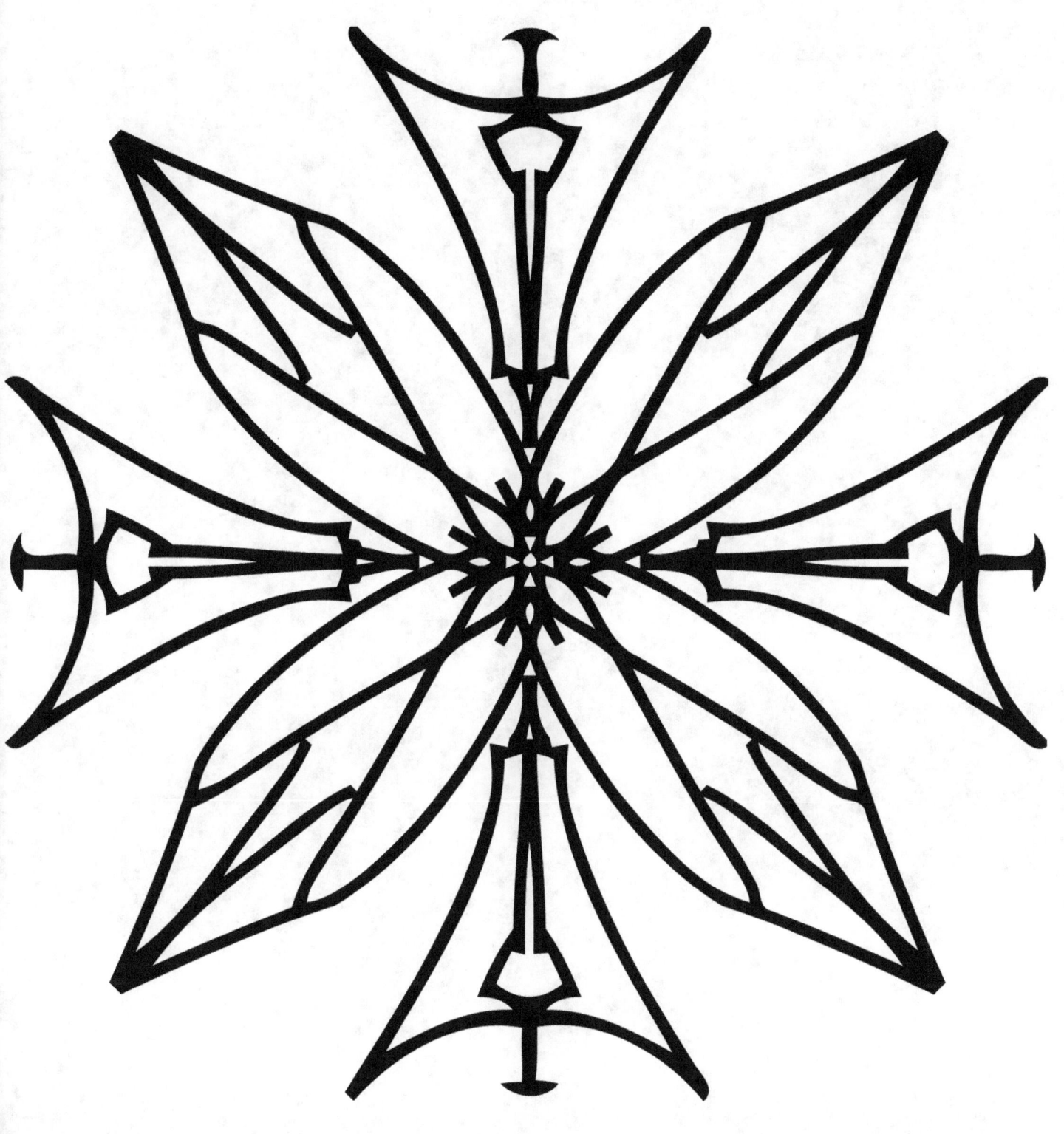

Illustrated by #cherylcolors
www.facebook.com/cherylcolors

Colored by: _____

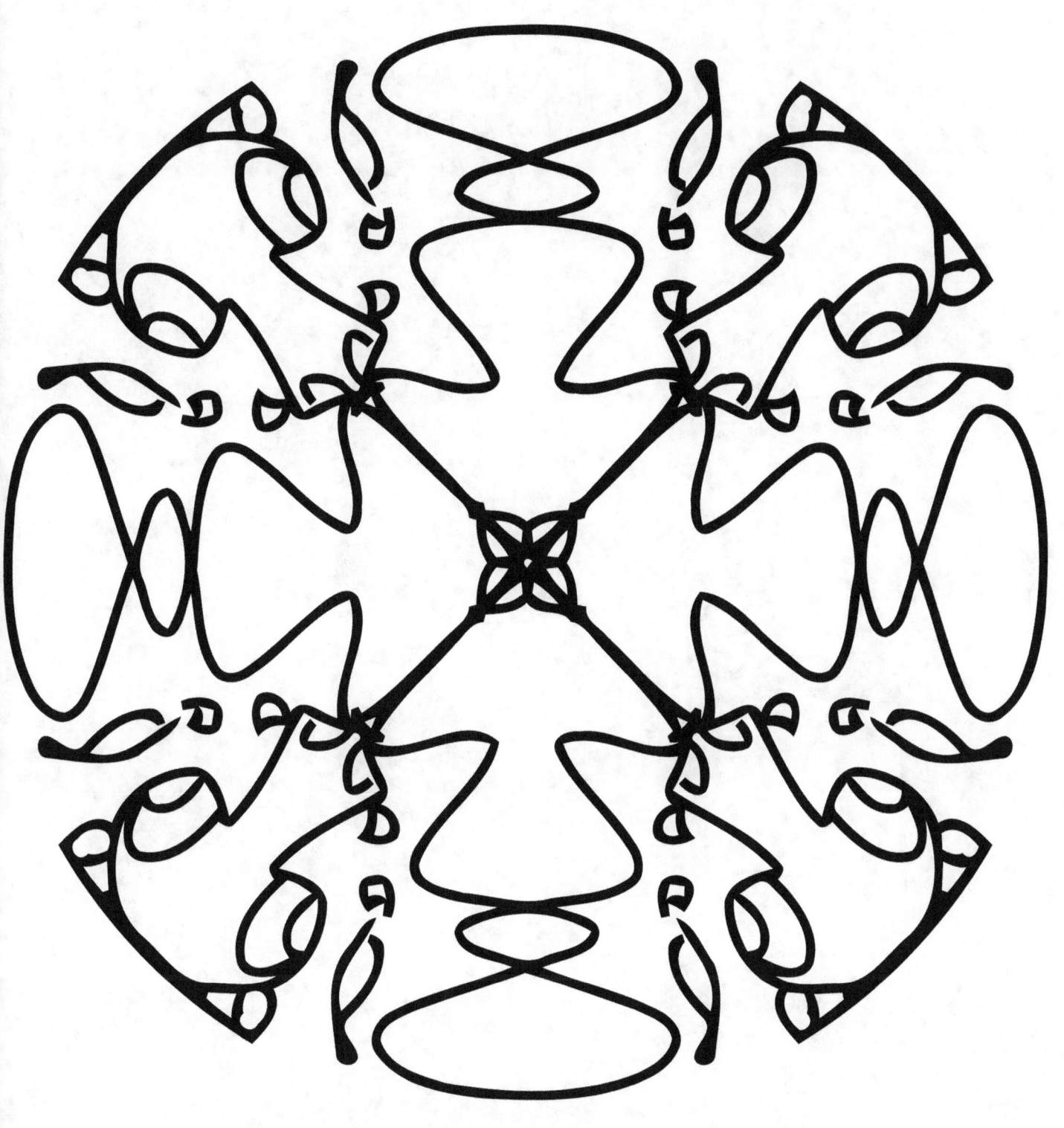

Illustrated by #cherylcolors
www.facebook.com/cherylcolors

Colored by: _____

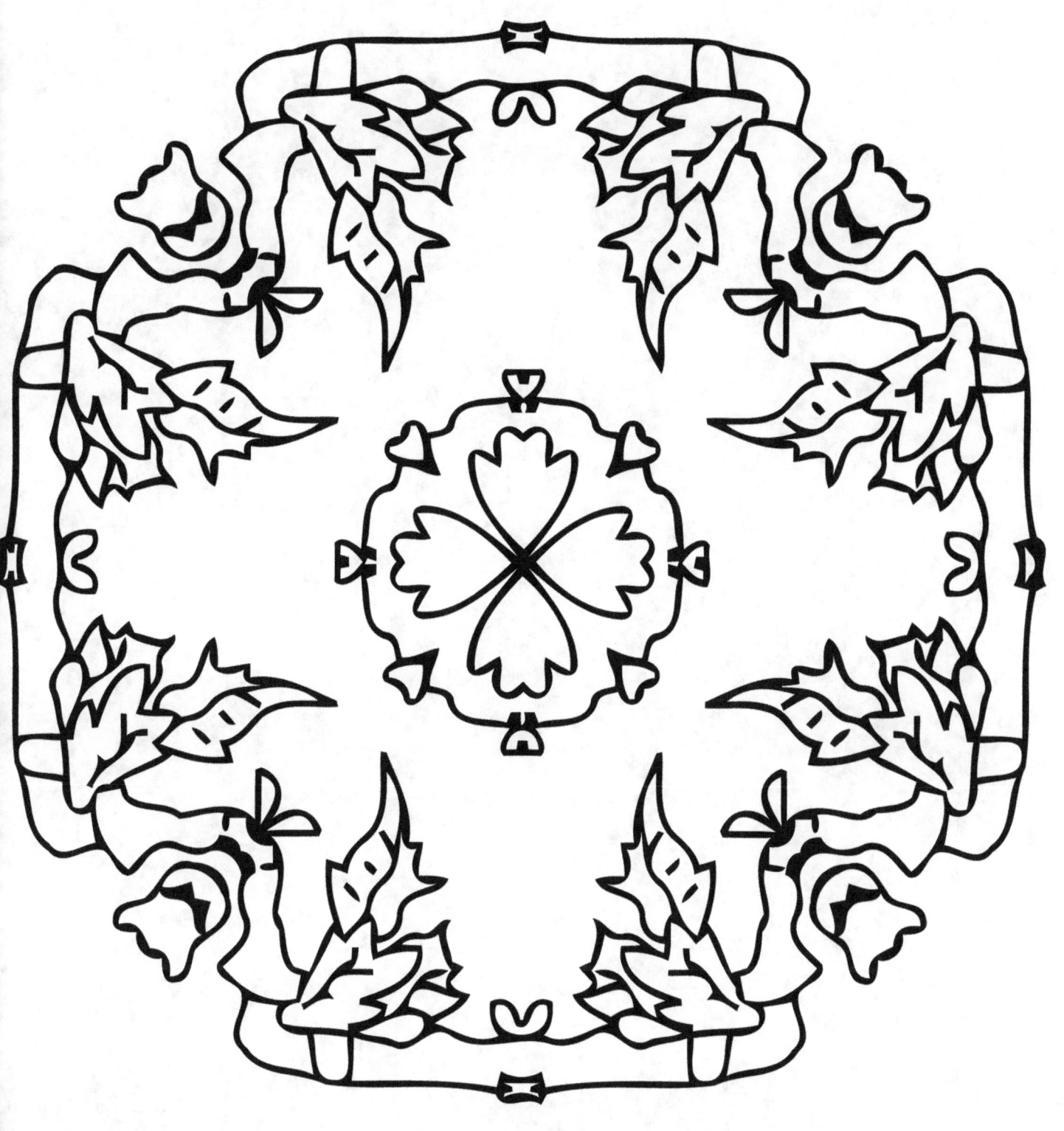

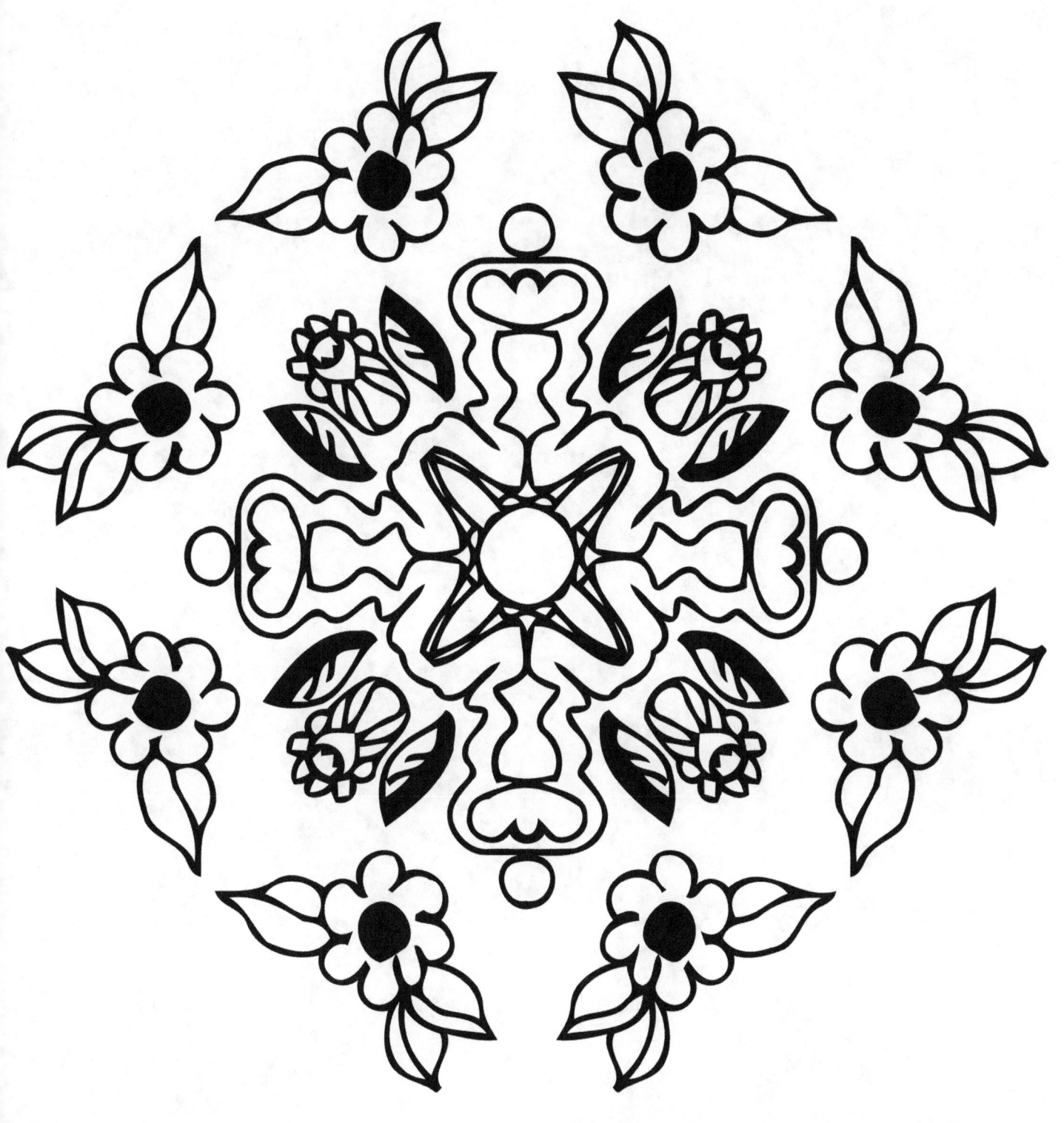

Illustrated by #cherylcolors
www.facebook.com/cherylcolors

Colored by: _____

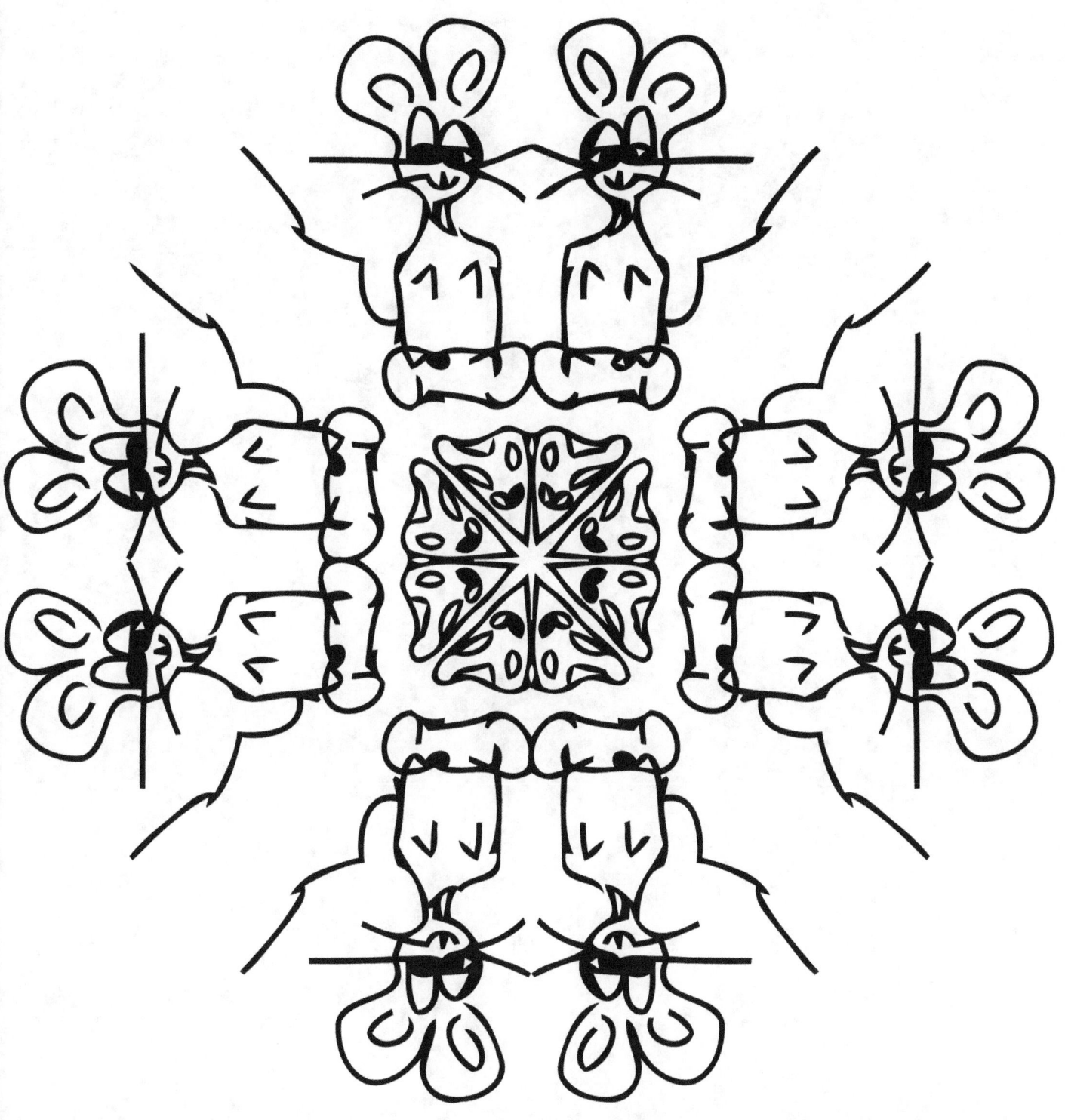

Illustrated by #cherylcolors
www.facebook.com/cherylcolors

Colored by: _____

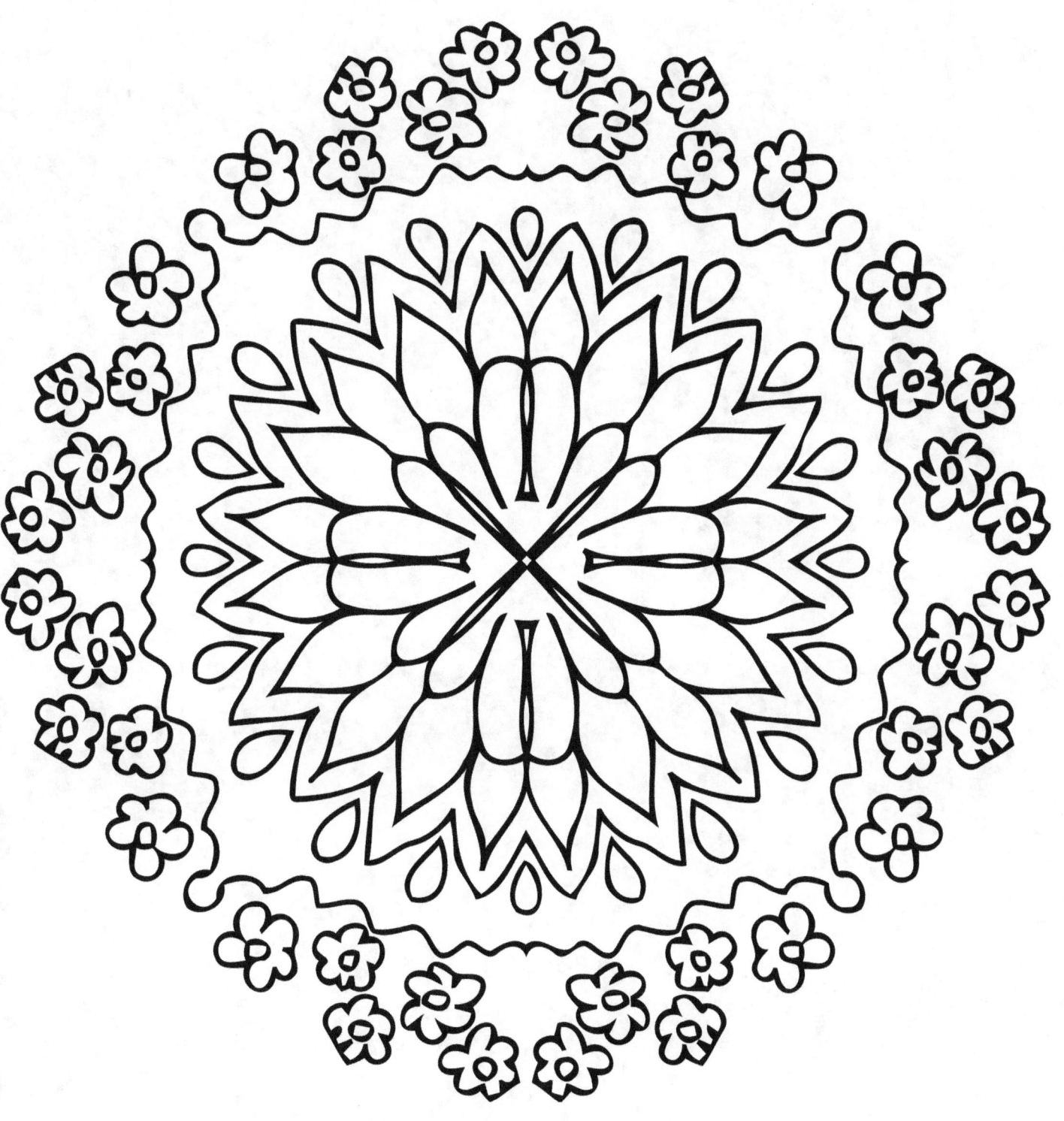

Illustrated by #cherylcolors
www.facebook.com/cherylcolors

Colored by: _____

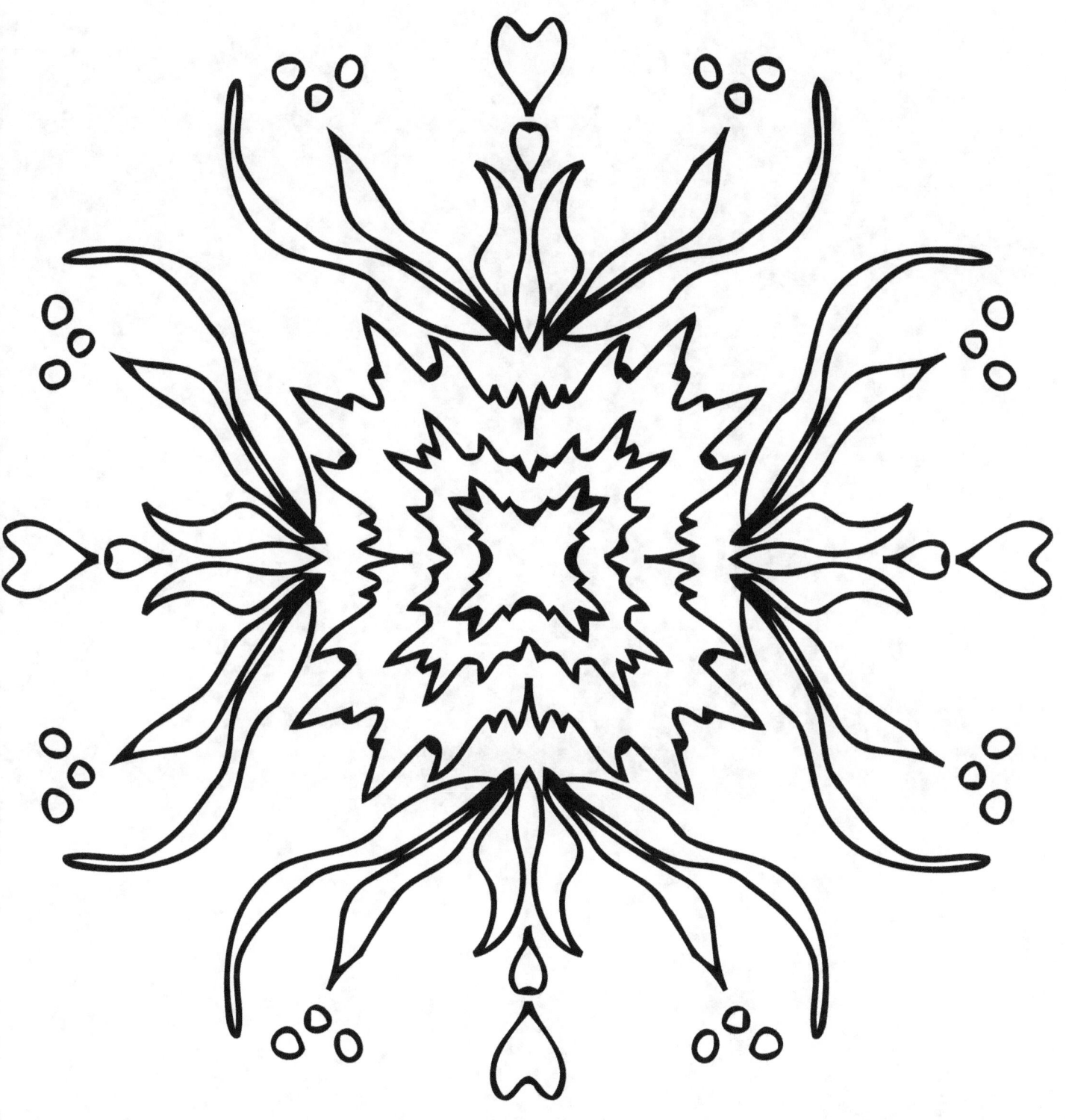

Illustrated by #cherylcolors
www.facebook.com/cherylcolors

Colored by: _____

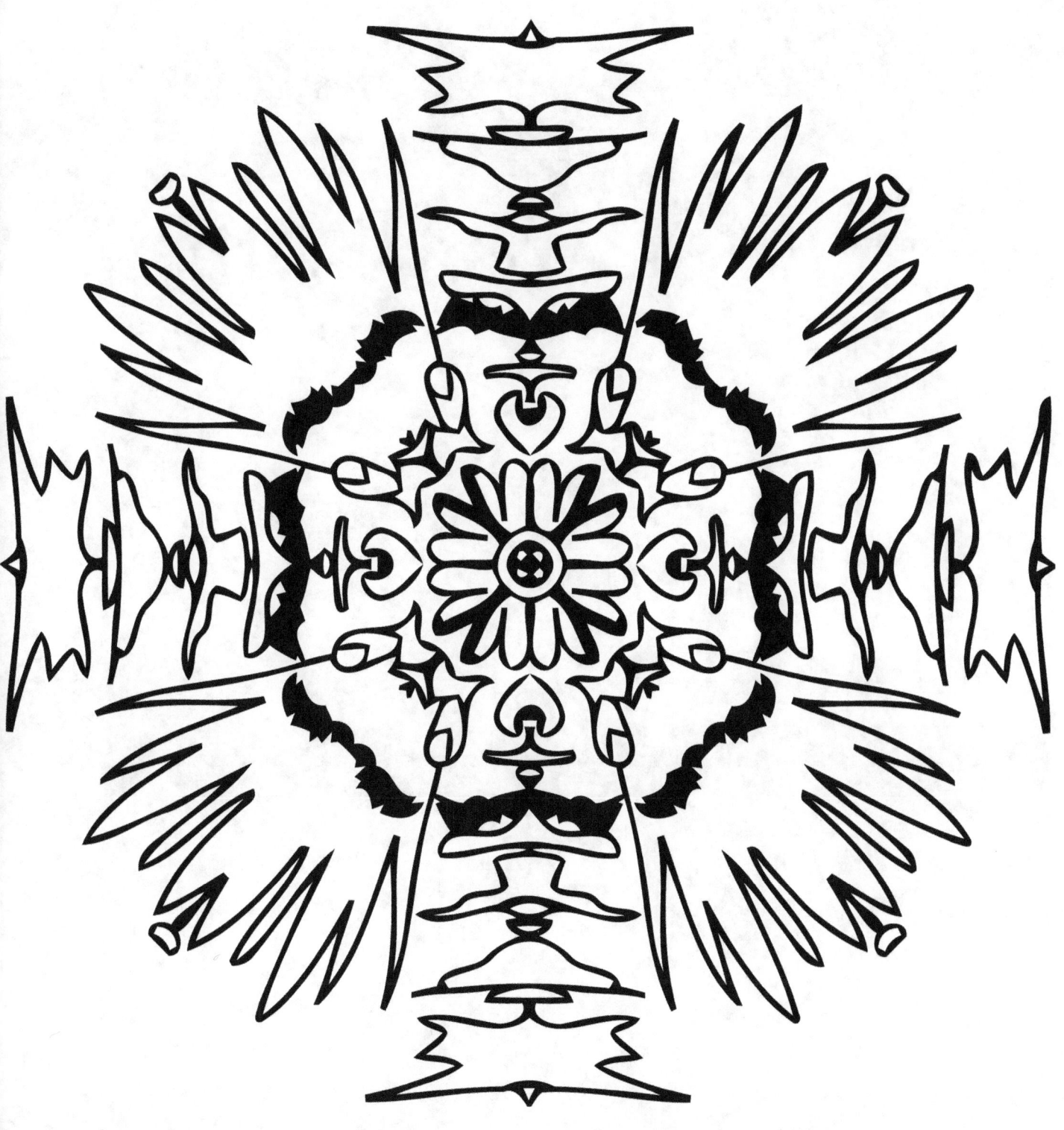

Illustrated by #cherylcolors
www.facebook.com/cherylcolors

Colored by: _____

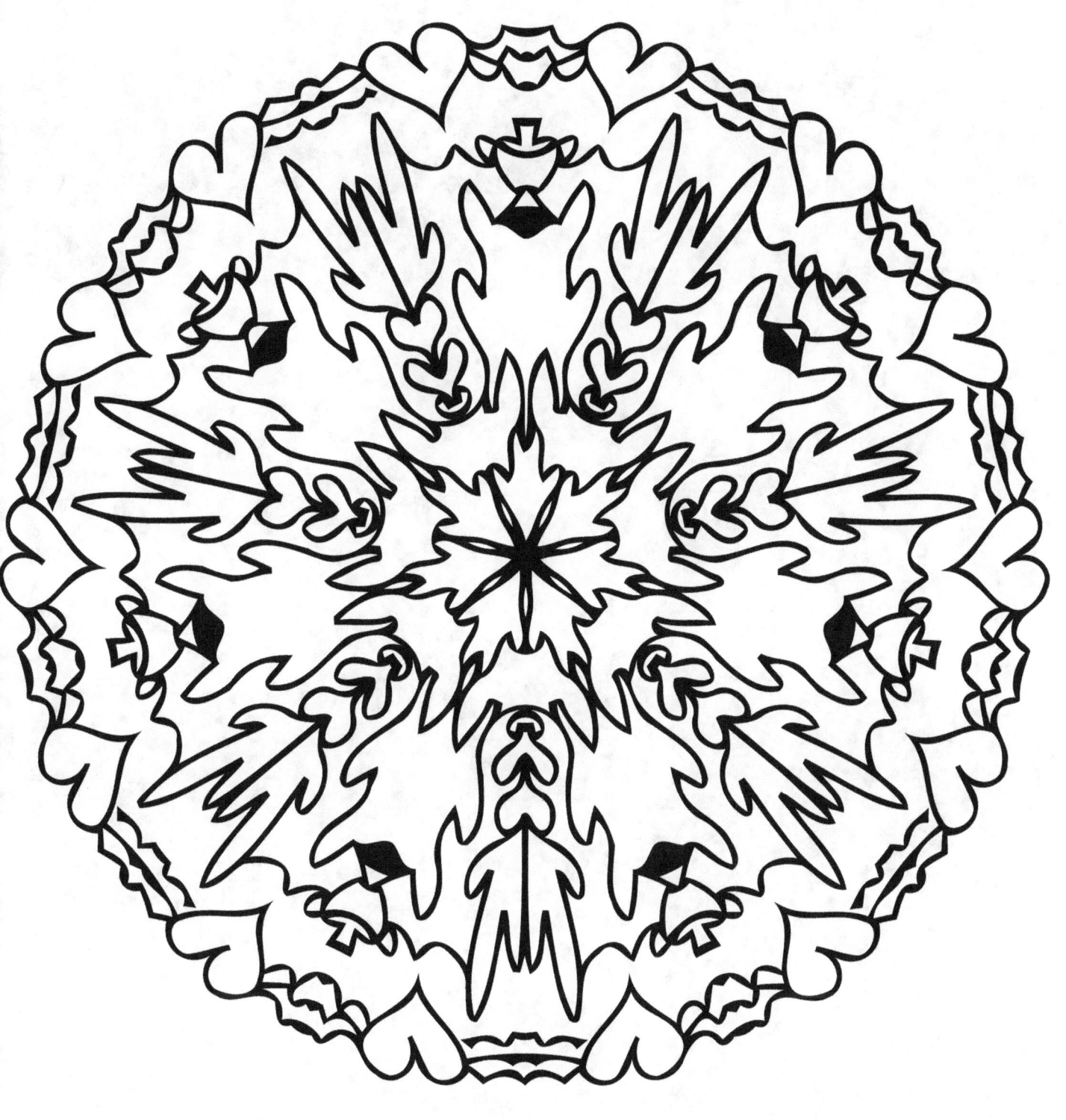

Illustrated by #cherylcolors
www.facebook.com/cherylcolors

Colored by: _____

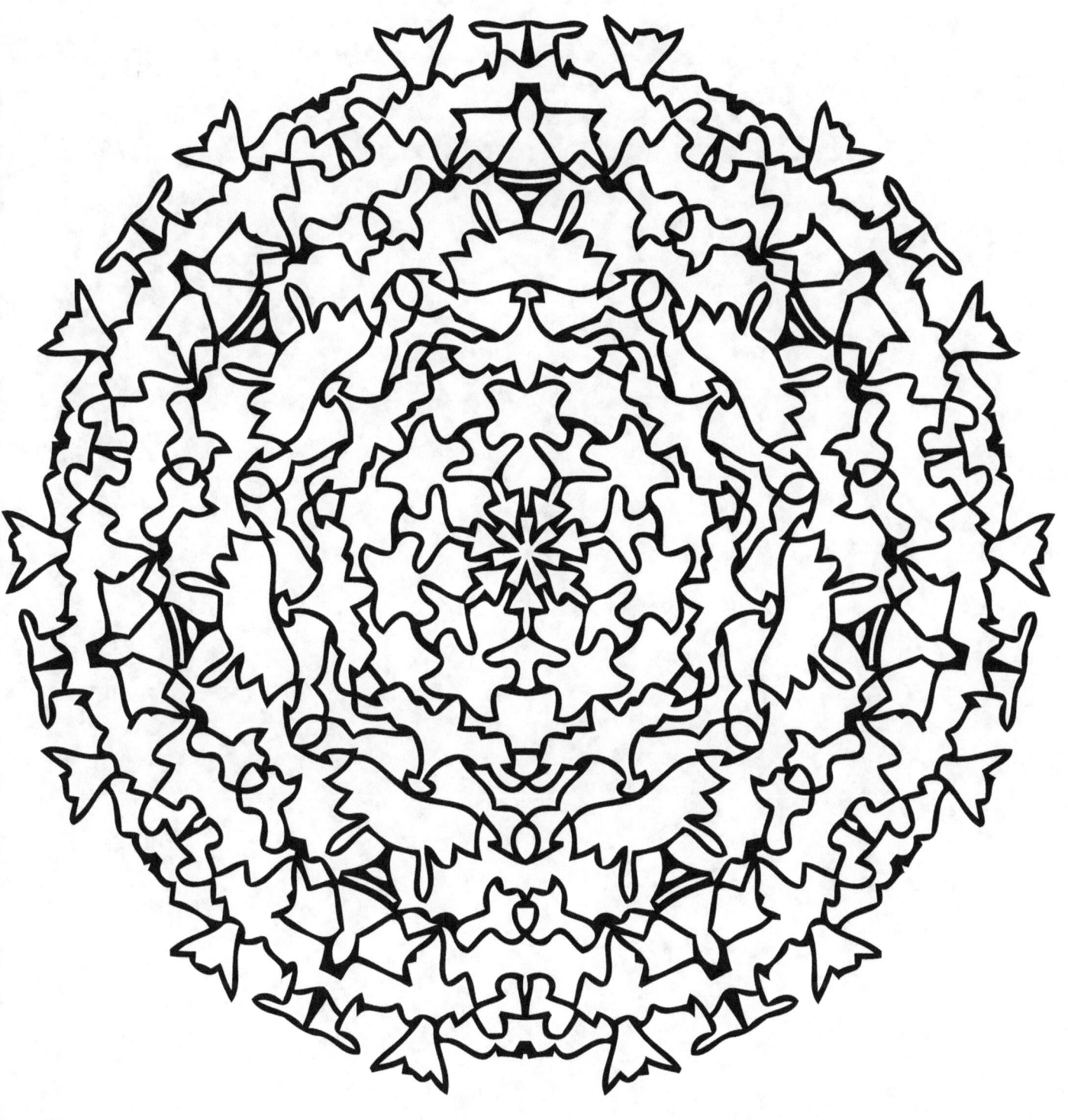

Illustrated by #cherylcolors
www.facebook.com/cherylcolors

Colored by: _____

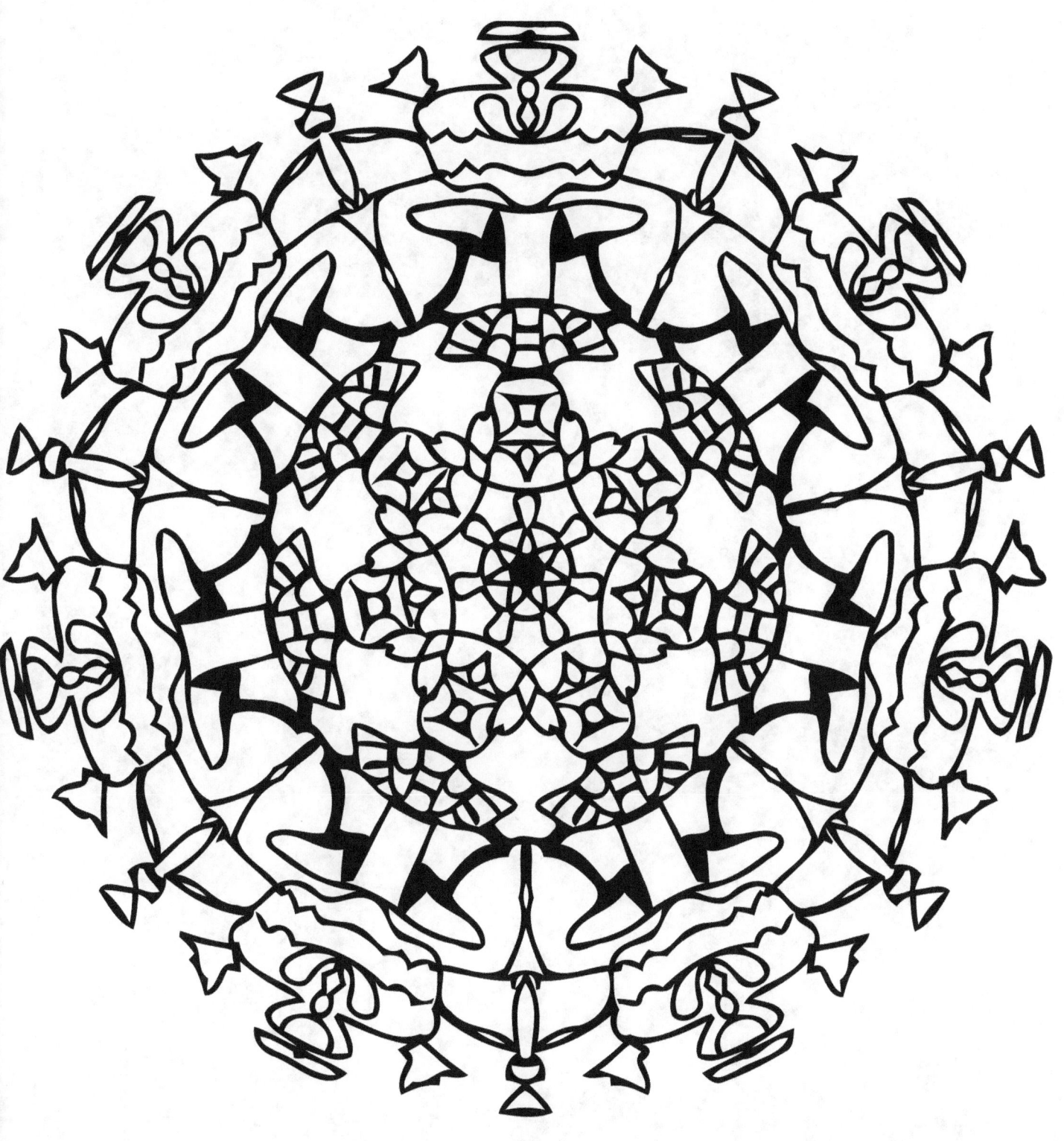

Illustrated by #cherylcolors
www.facebook.com/cherylcolors

Colored by: _____

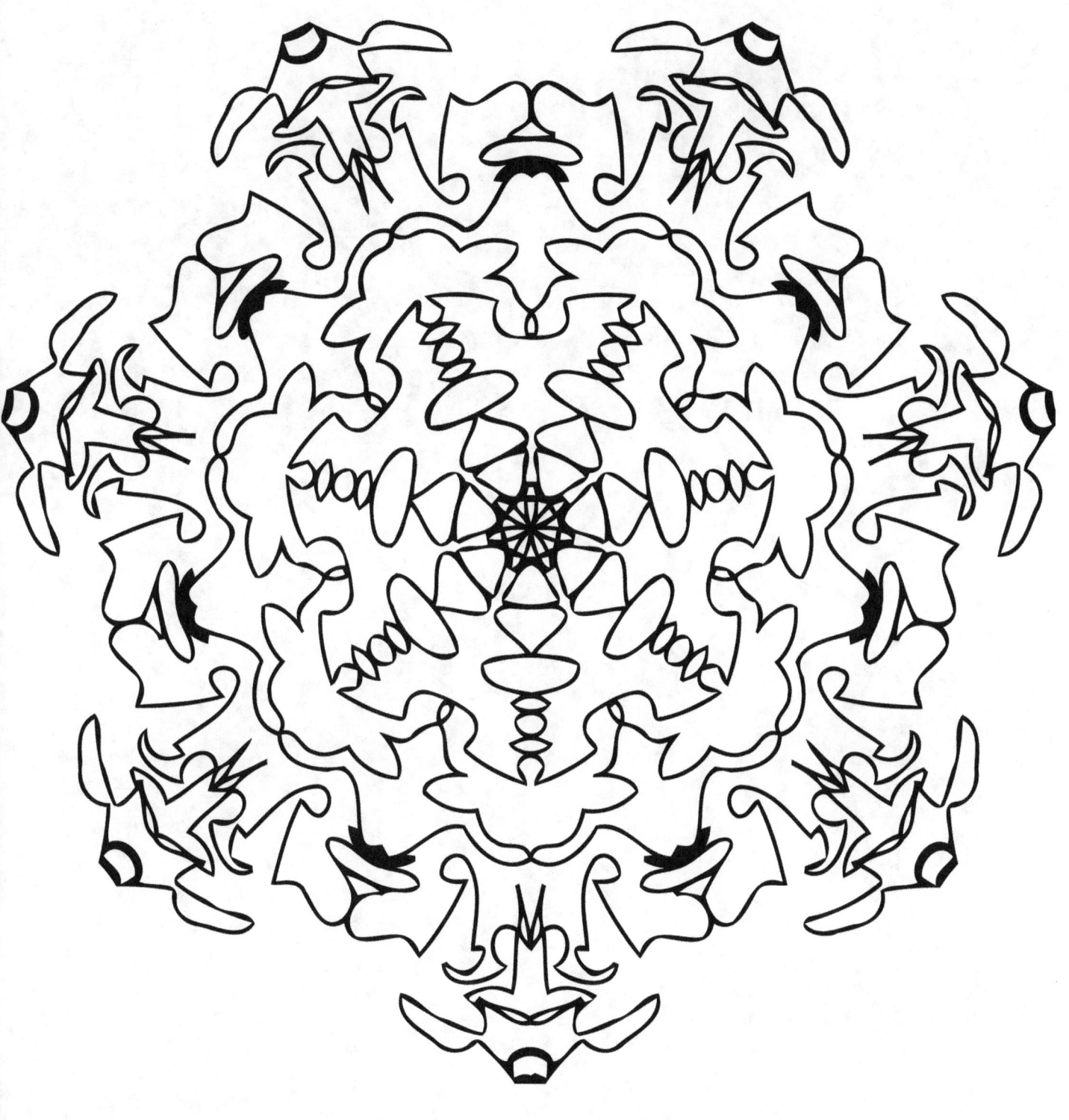

Illustrated by #cherylcolors
www.facebook.com/cherylcolors

Colored by: _____

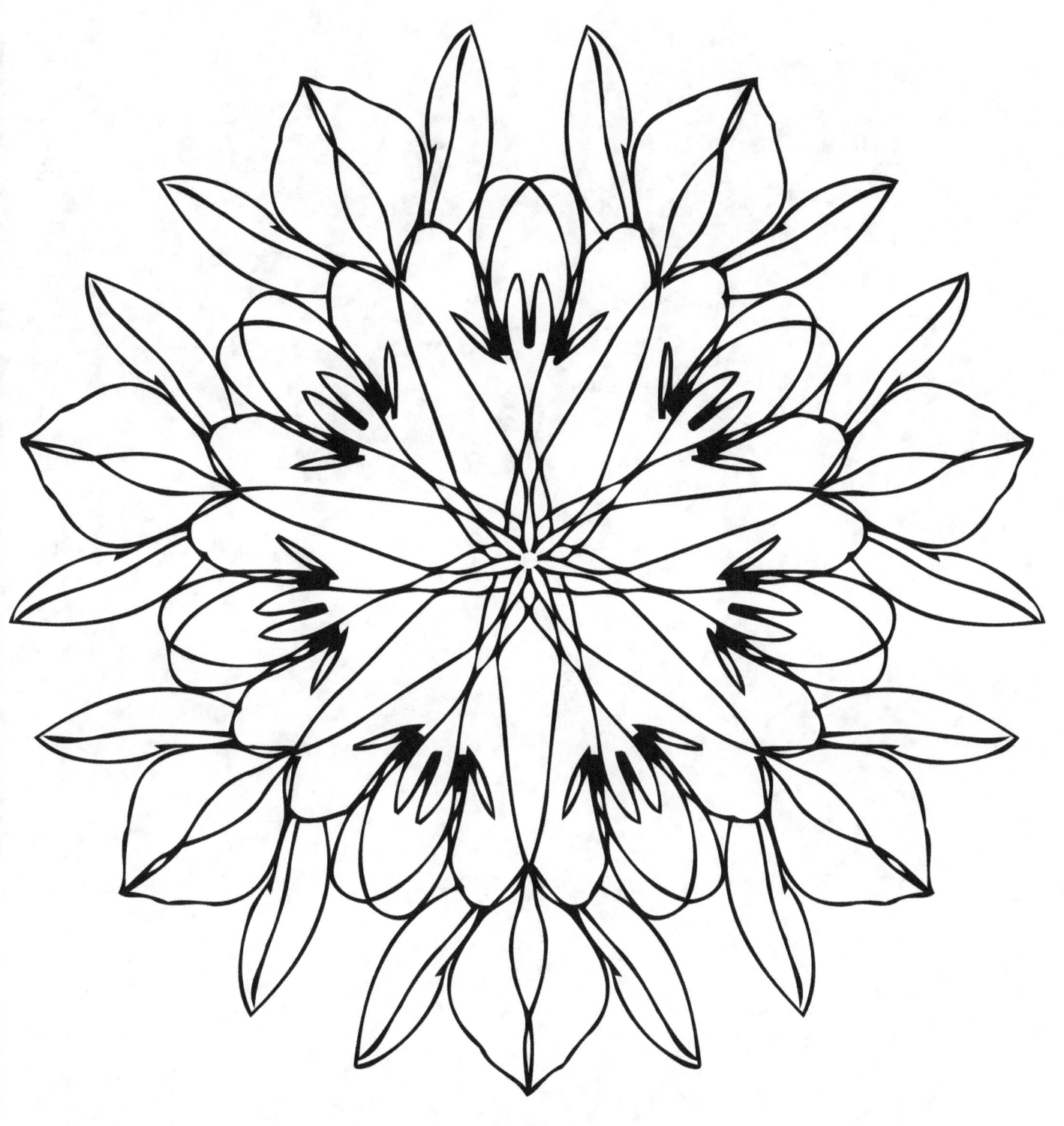

Illustrated by #cherylcolors
www.facebook.com/cherylcolors

Colored by: _____

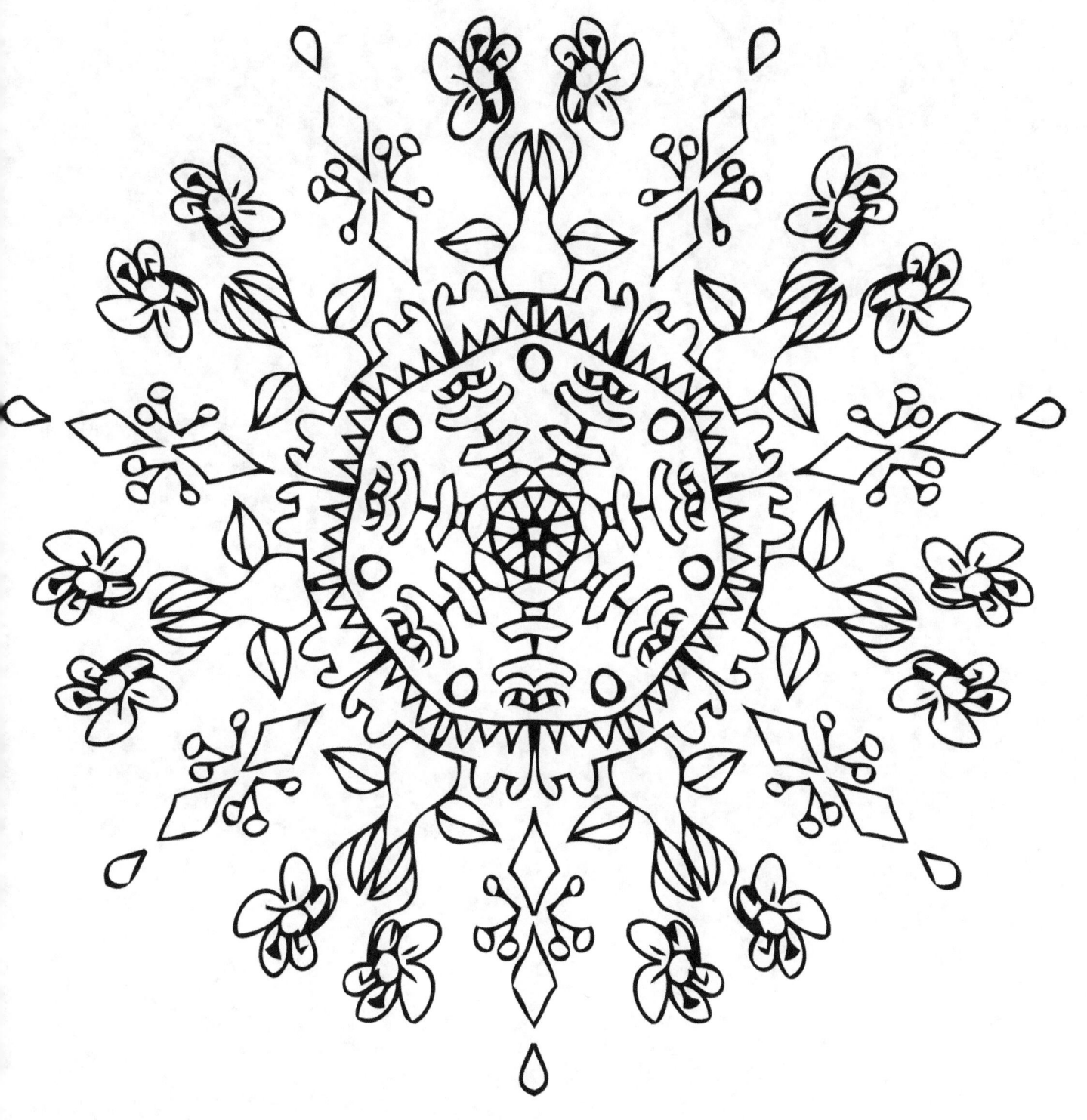

Illustrated by #cherylcolors
www.facebook.com/cherylcolors

Colored by: _____

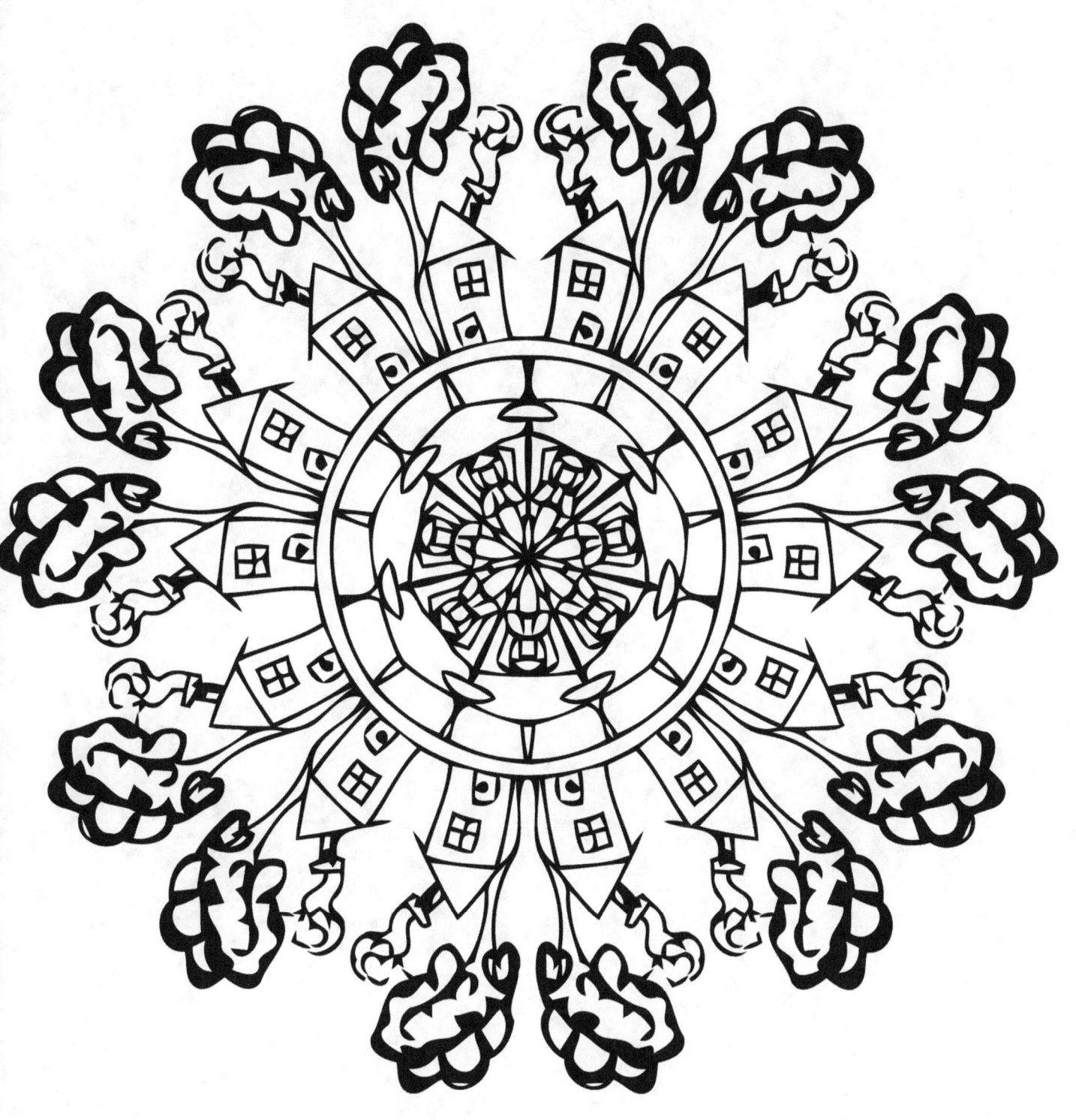

Illustrated by #cherylcolors
www.facebook.com/cherylcolors

Colored by: _____

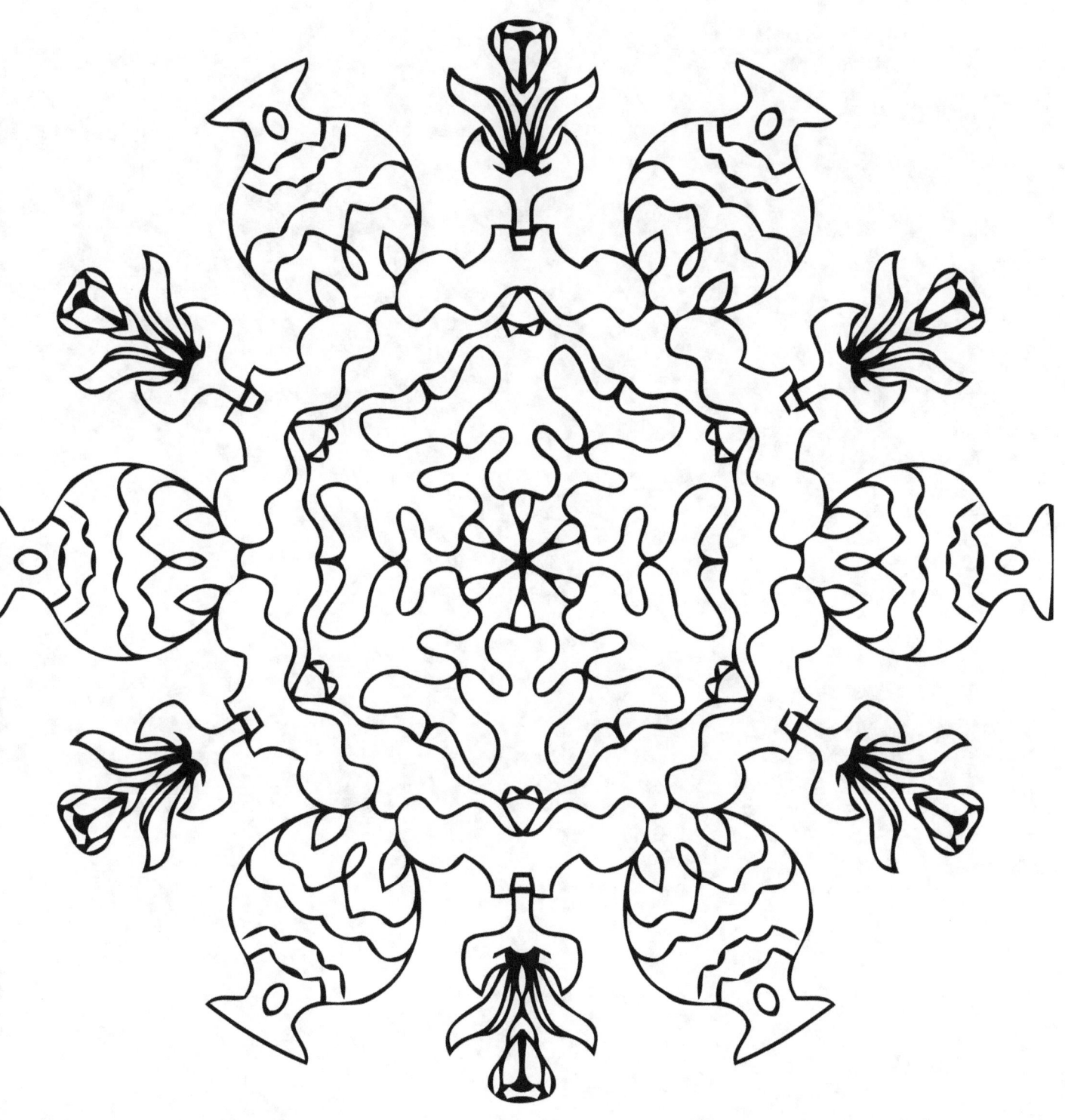

Illustrated by #cherylcolors
www.facebook.com/cherylcolors

Colored by: _____

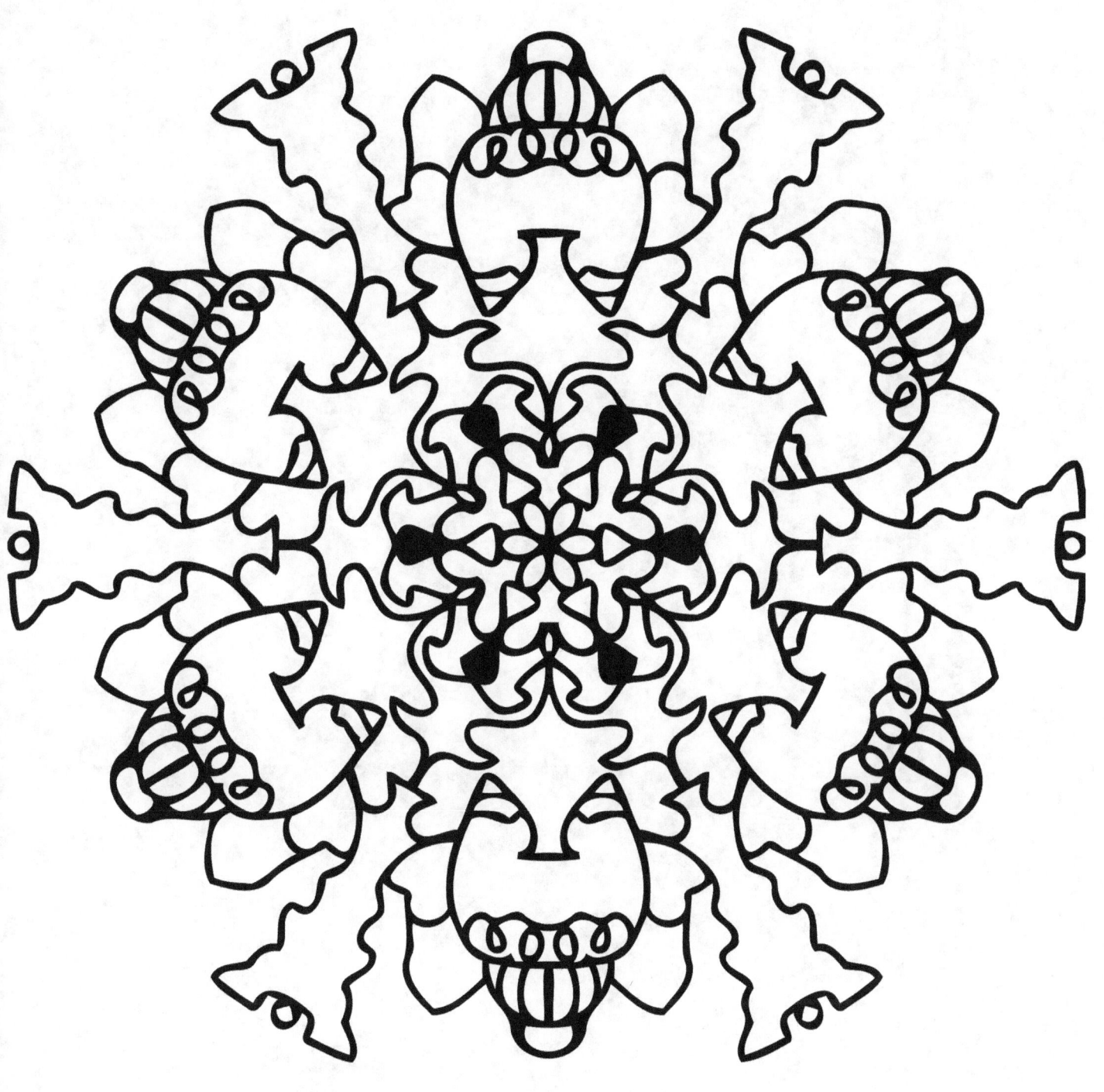

Illustrated by #cherylcolors
www.facebook.com/cherylcolors

Colored by: _____

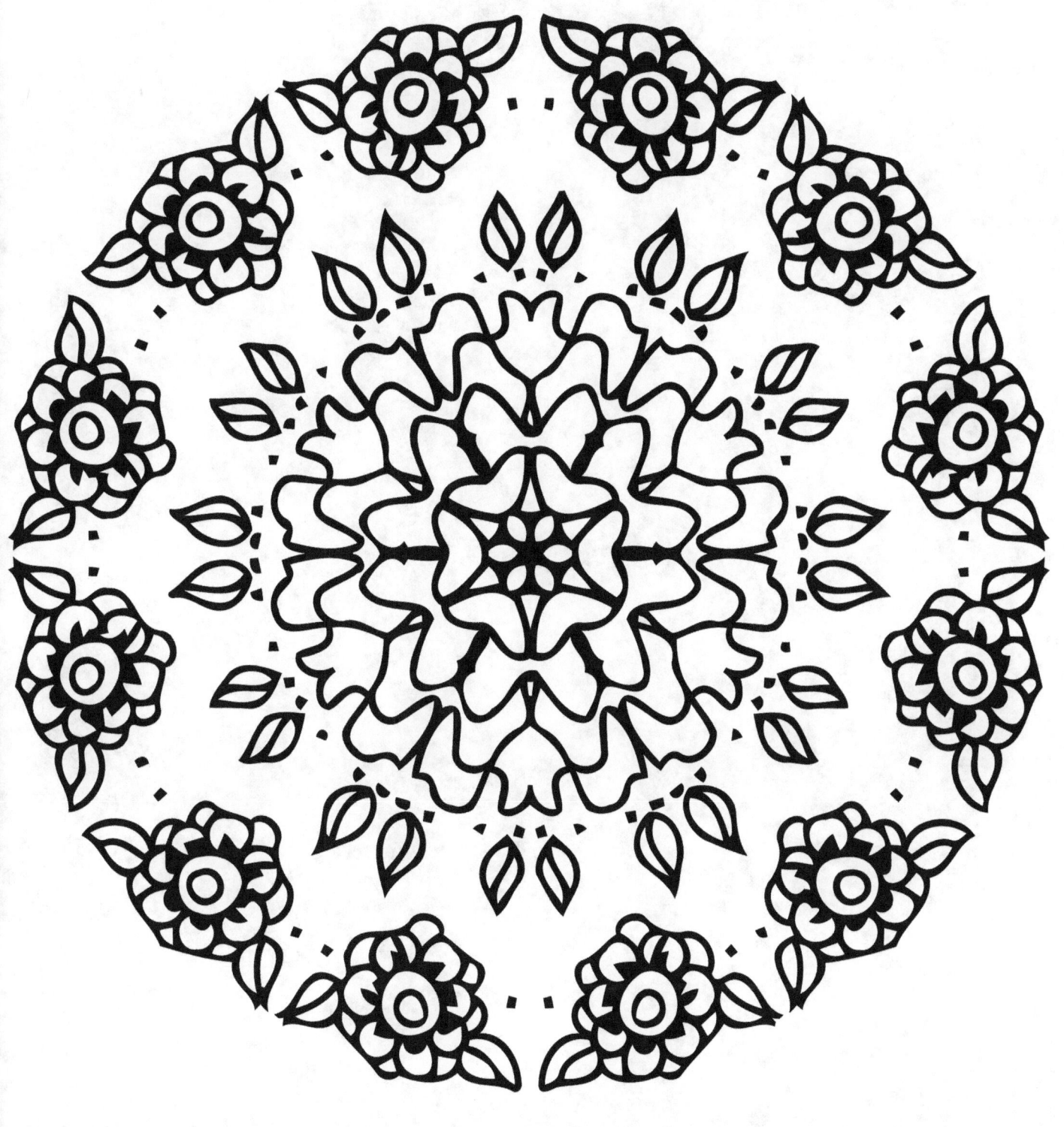

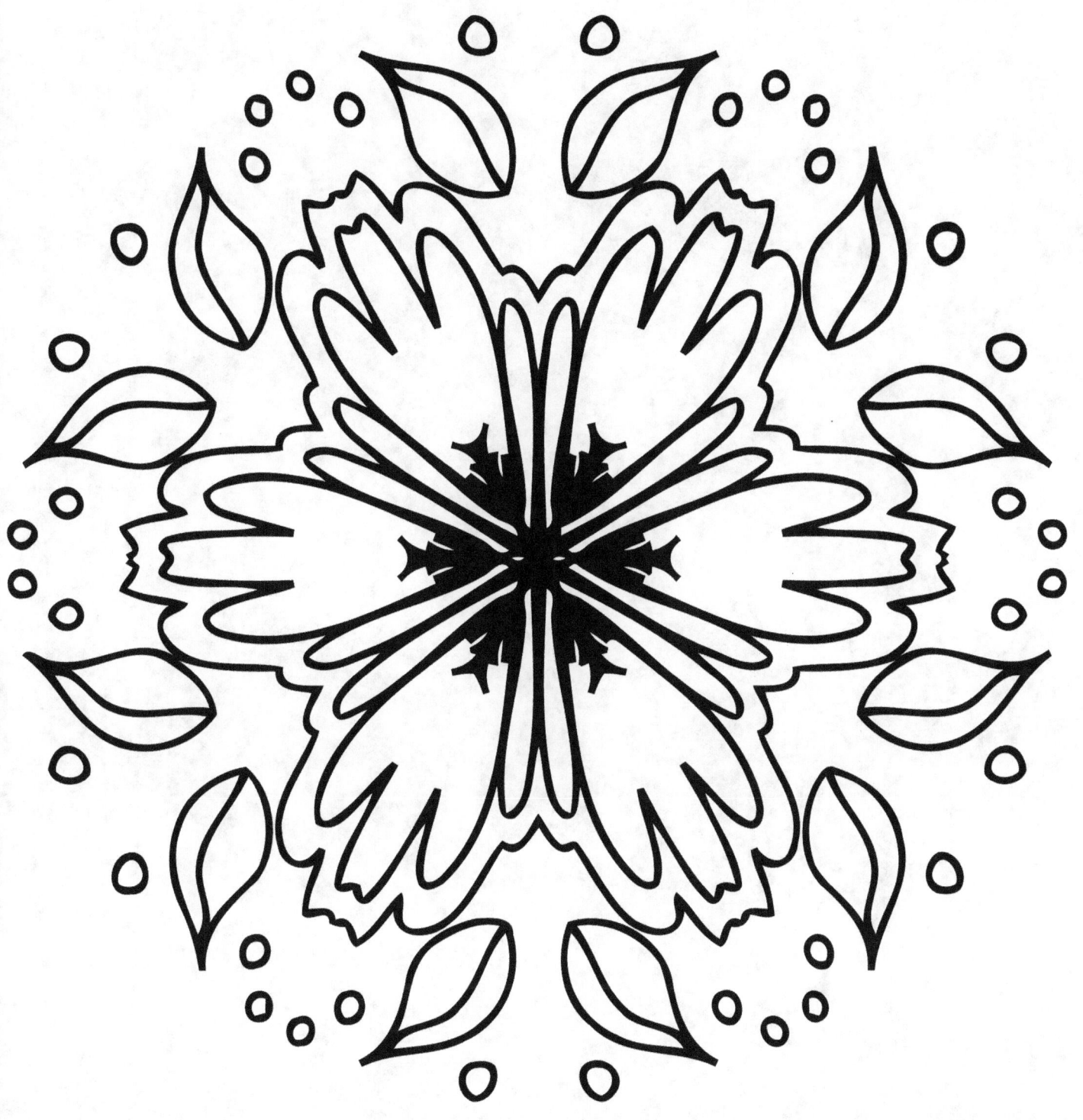

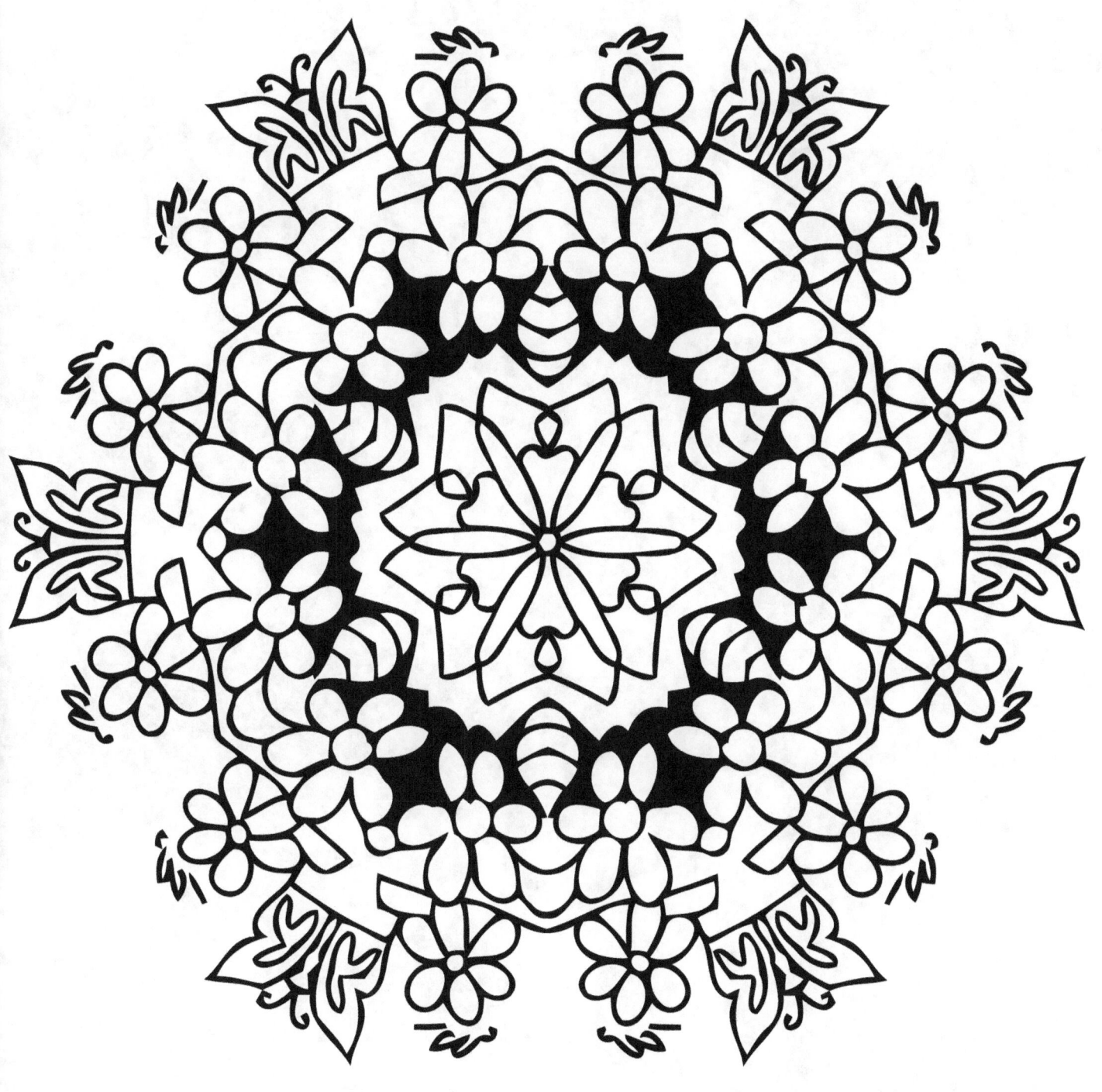

Illustrated by #cherylcolors
www.facebook.com/cherylcolors

Colored by: _____

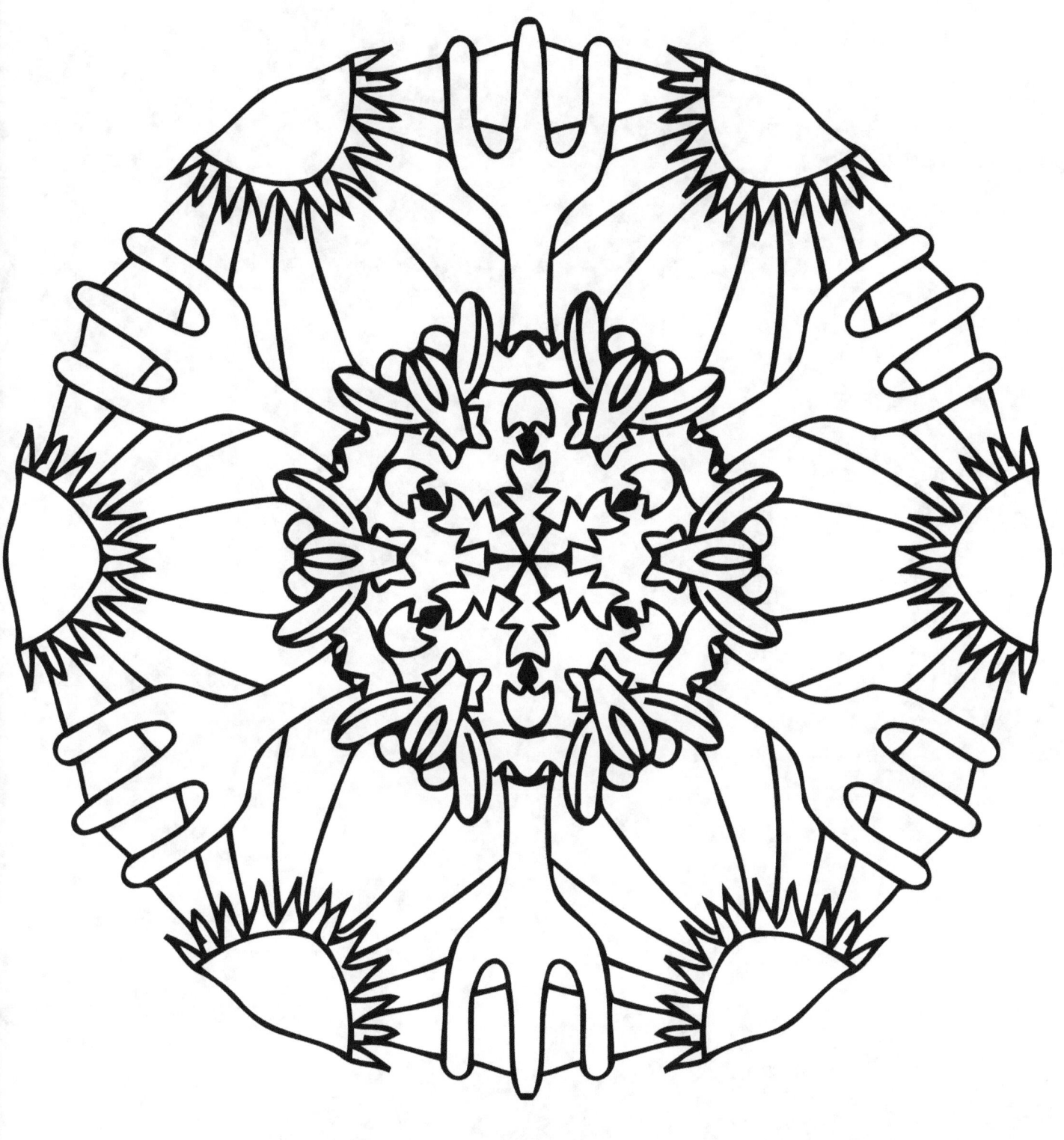

Illustrated by #cherylcolors
www.facebook.com/cherylcolors

Colored by: _____

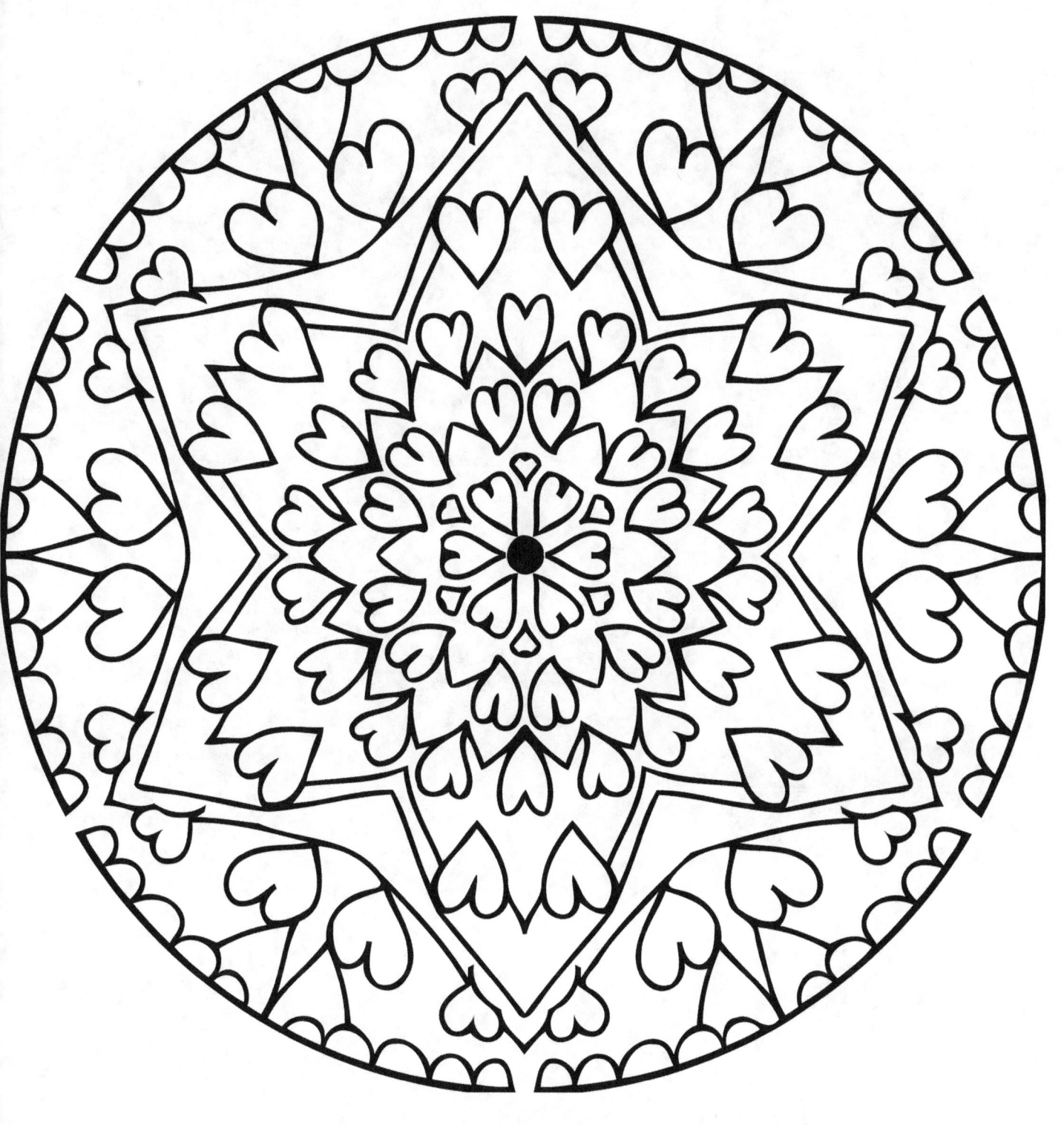

Illustrated by #cherylcolors
www.facebook.com/cherylcolors

Colored by: _____

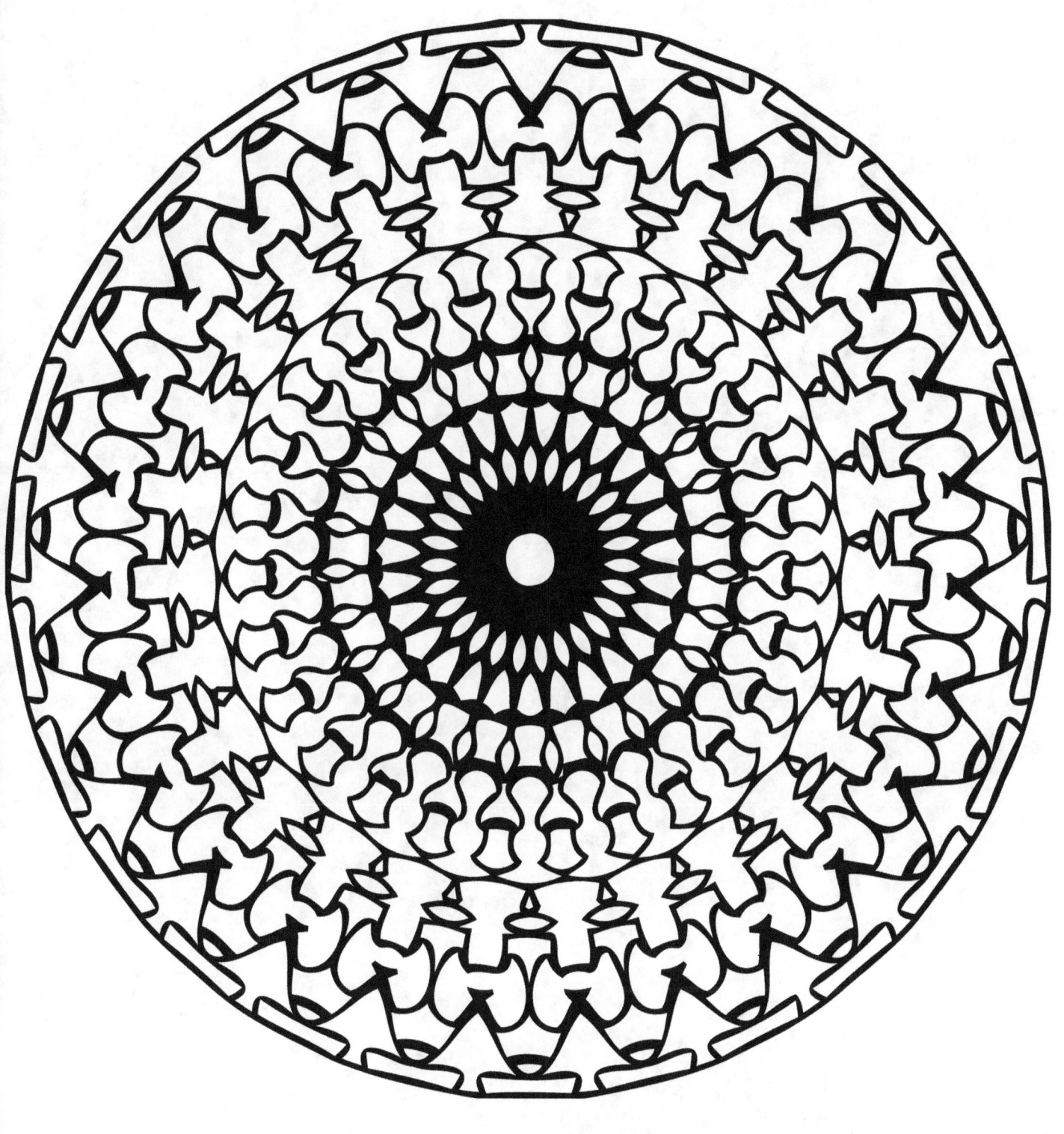

Illustrated by #cherylcolors
www.facebook.com/cherylcolors

Colored by: _____

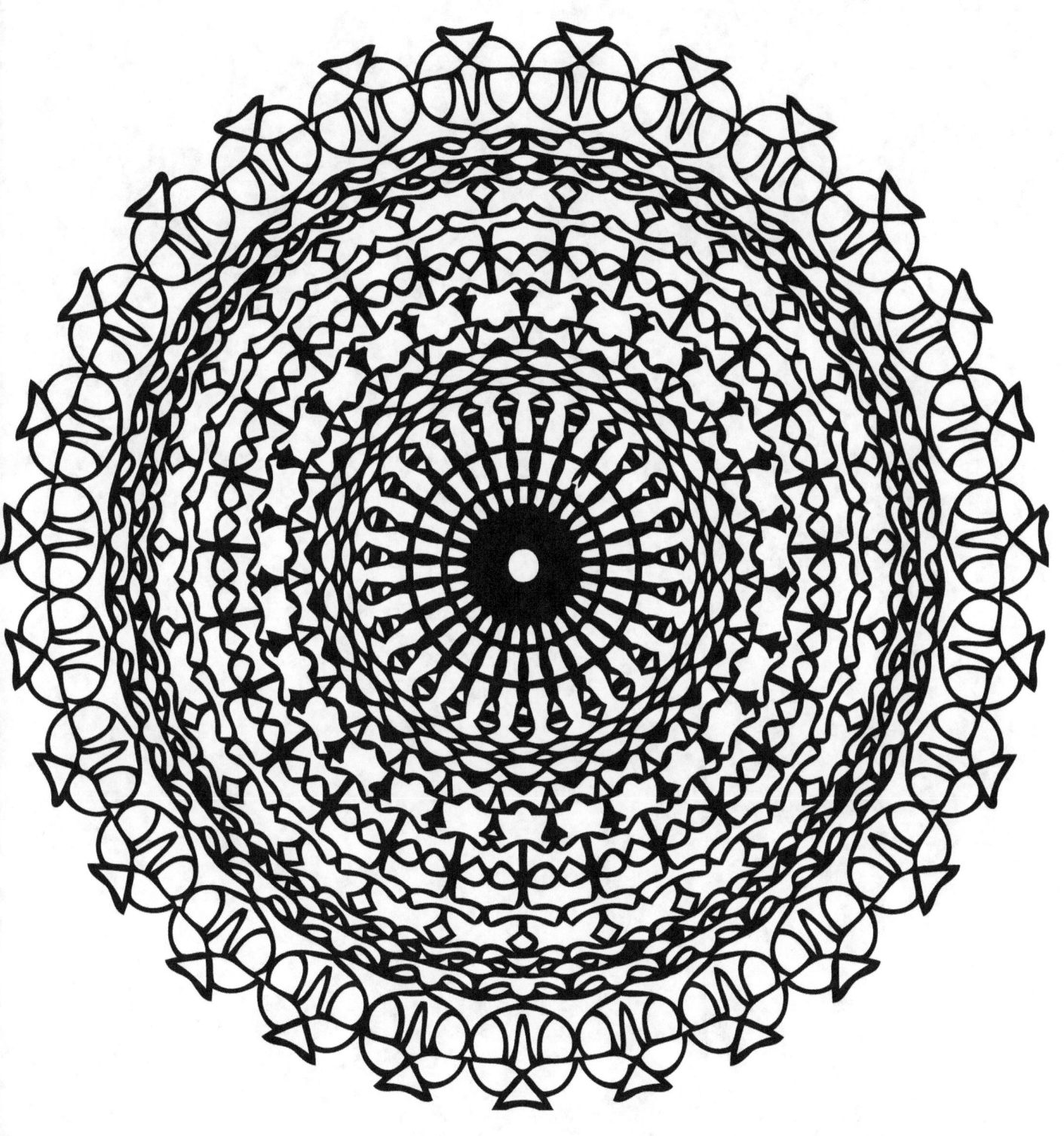

Illustrated by #cherylcolors
www.facebook.com/cherylcolors

Colored by: _____

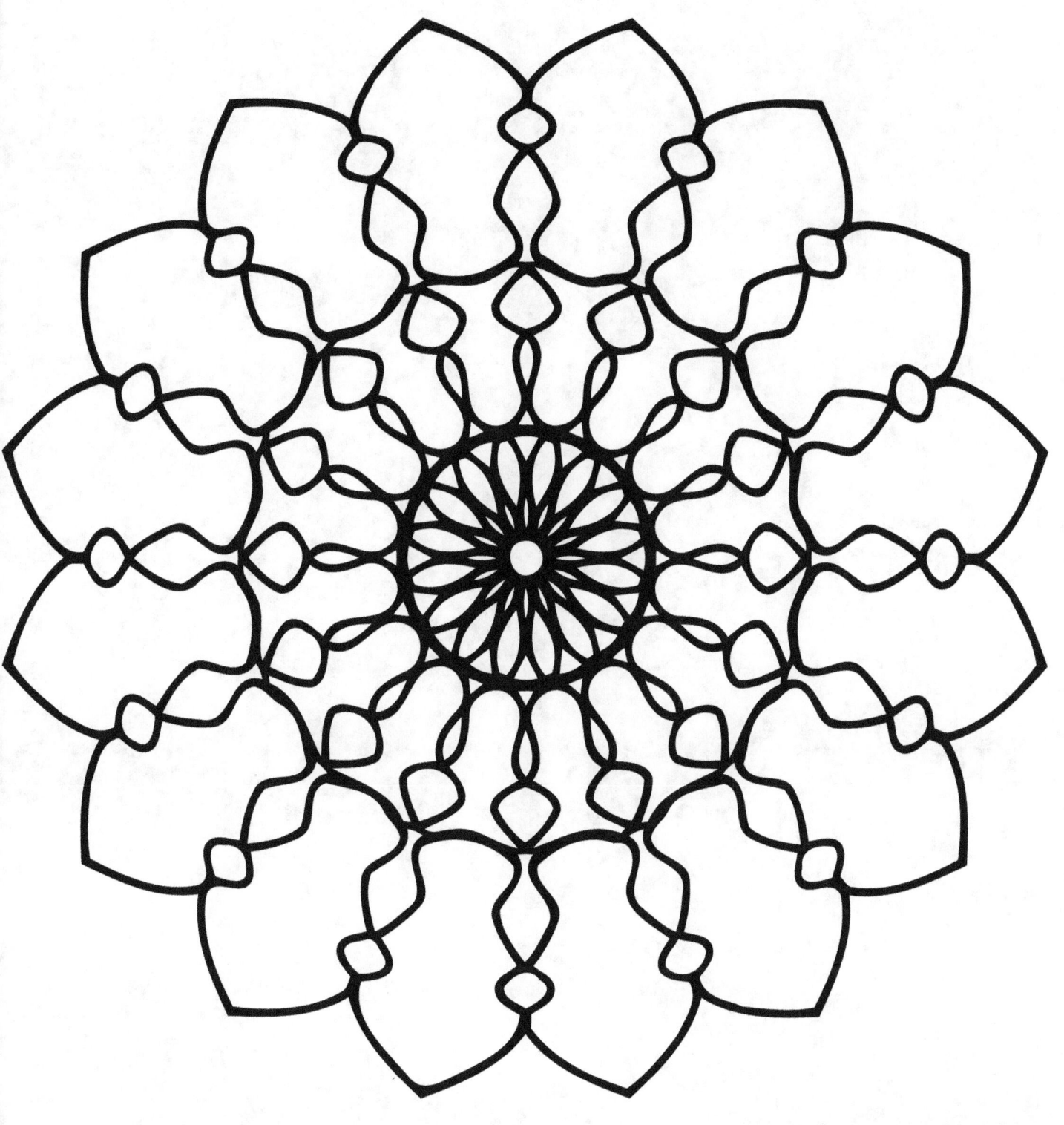

Illustrated by #cherylcolors
www.facebook.com/cherylcolors

Colored by: _____

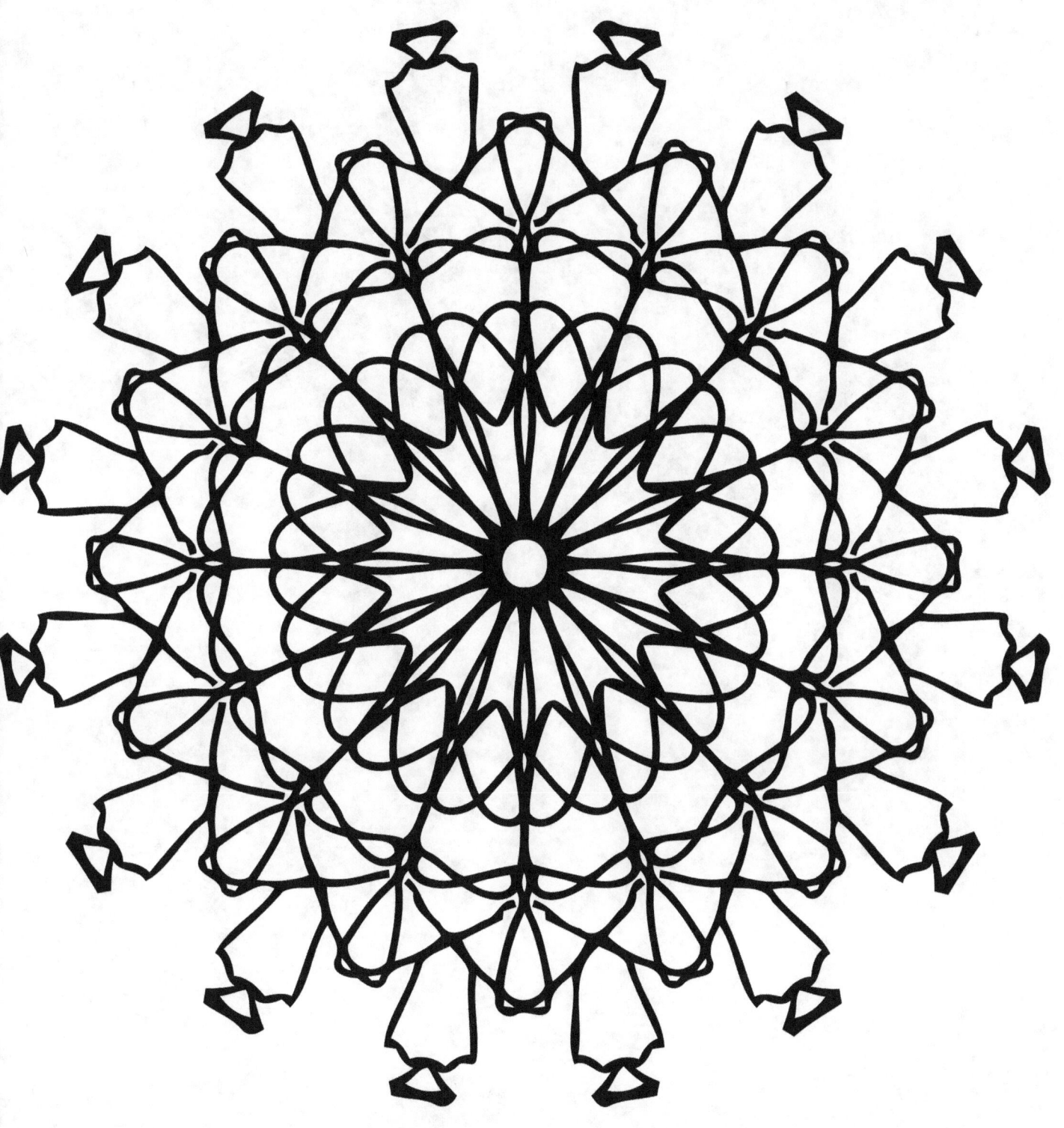

Illustrated by #cherylcolors
www.facebook.com/cherylcolors

Colored by: _____

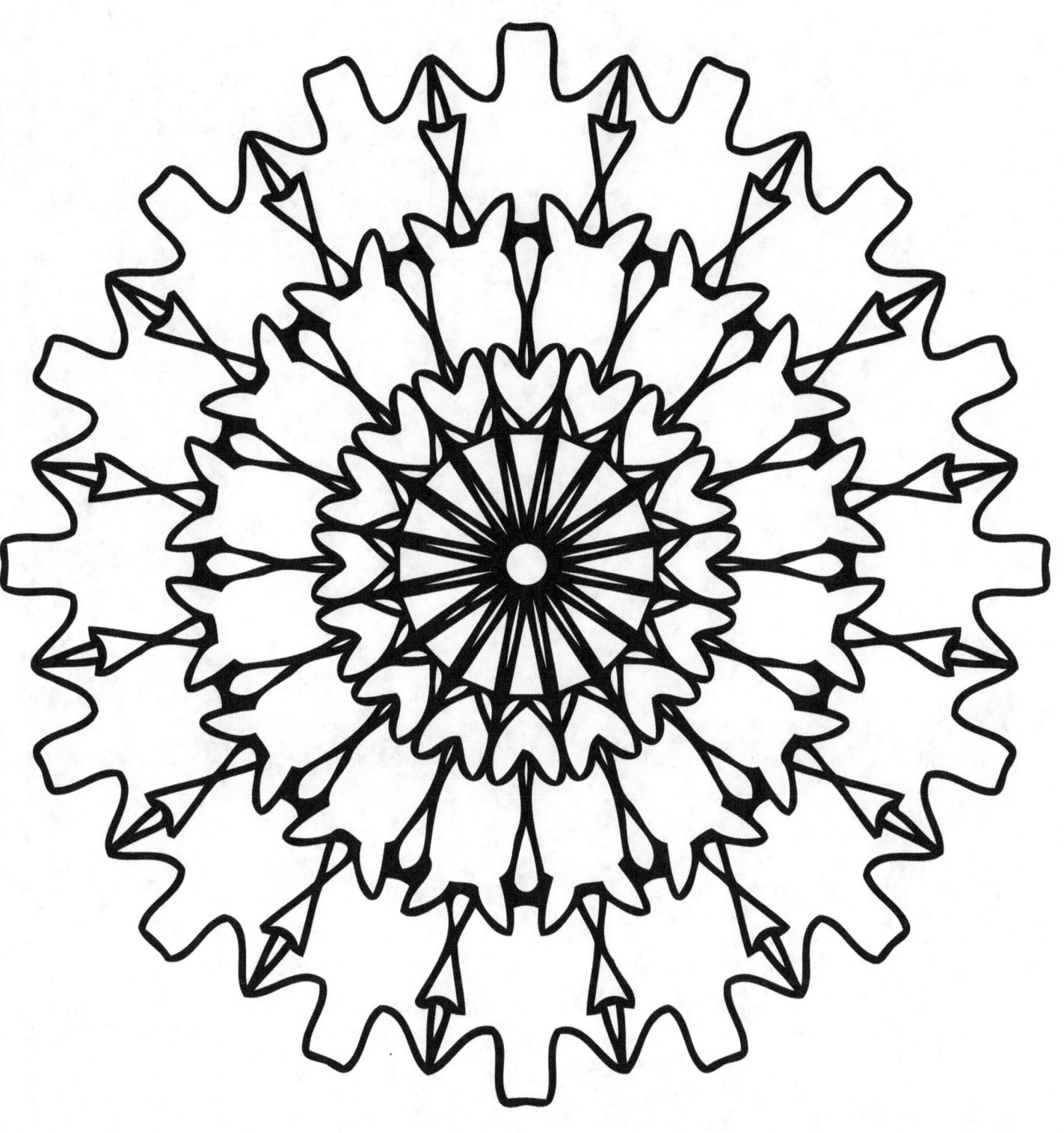

Illustrated by #cherylcolors
www.facebook.com/cherylcolors

Colored by: _____

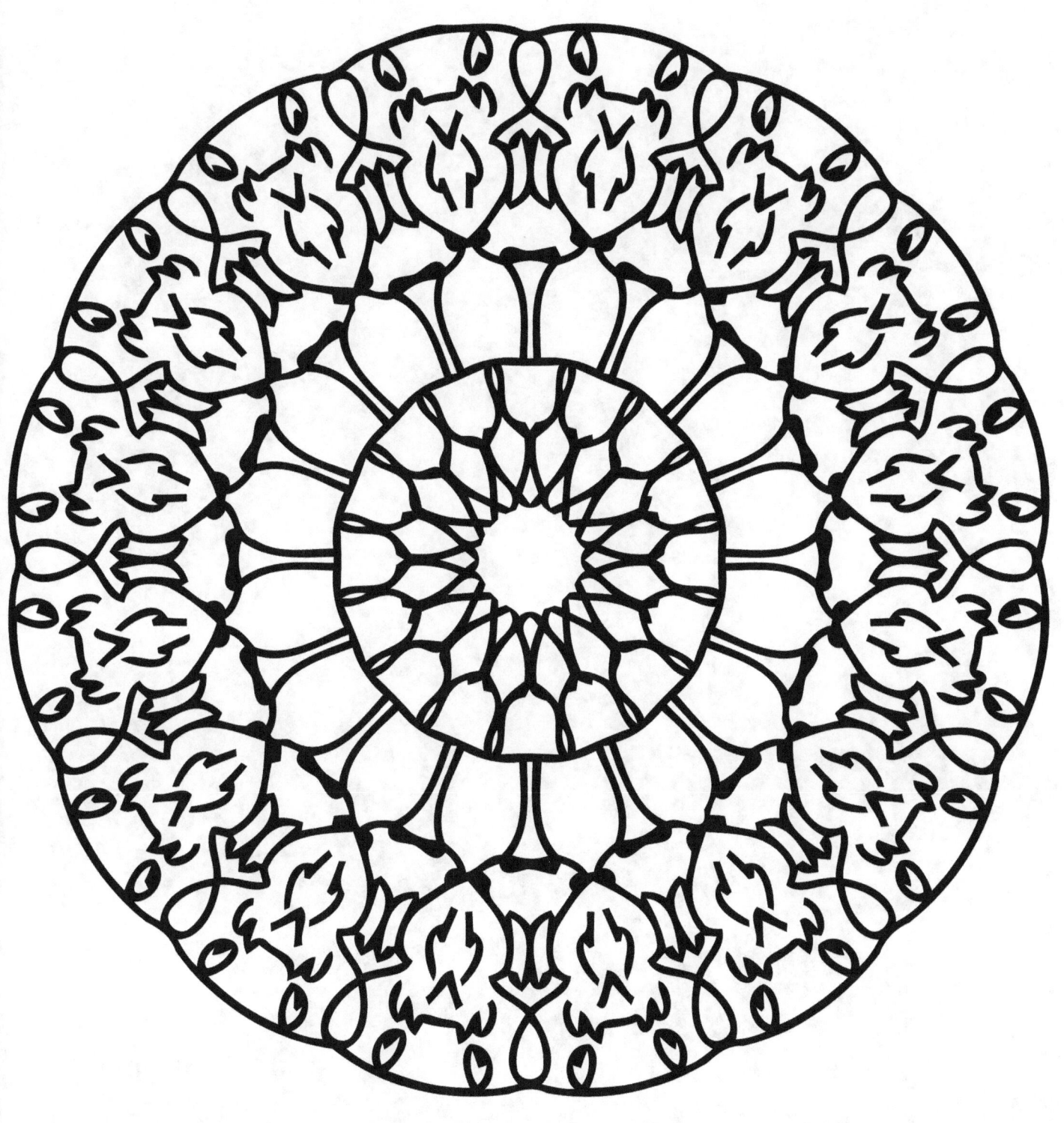

Illustrated by #cherylcolors
www.facebook.com/cherylcolors

Colored by: _____

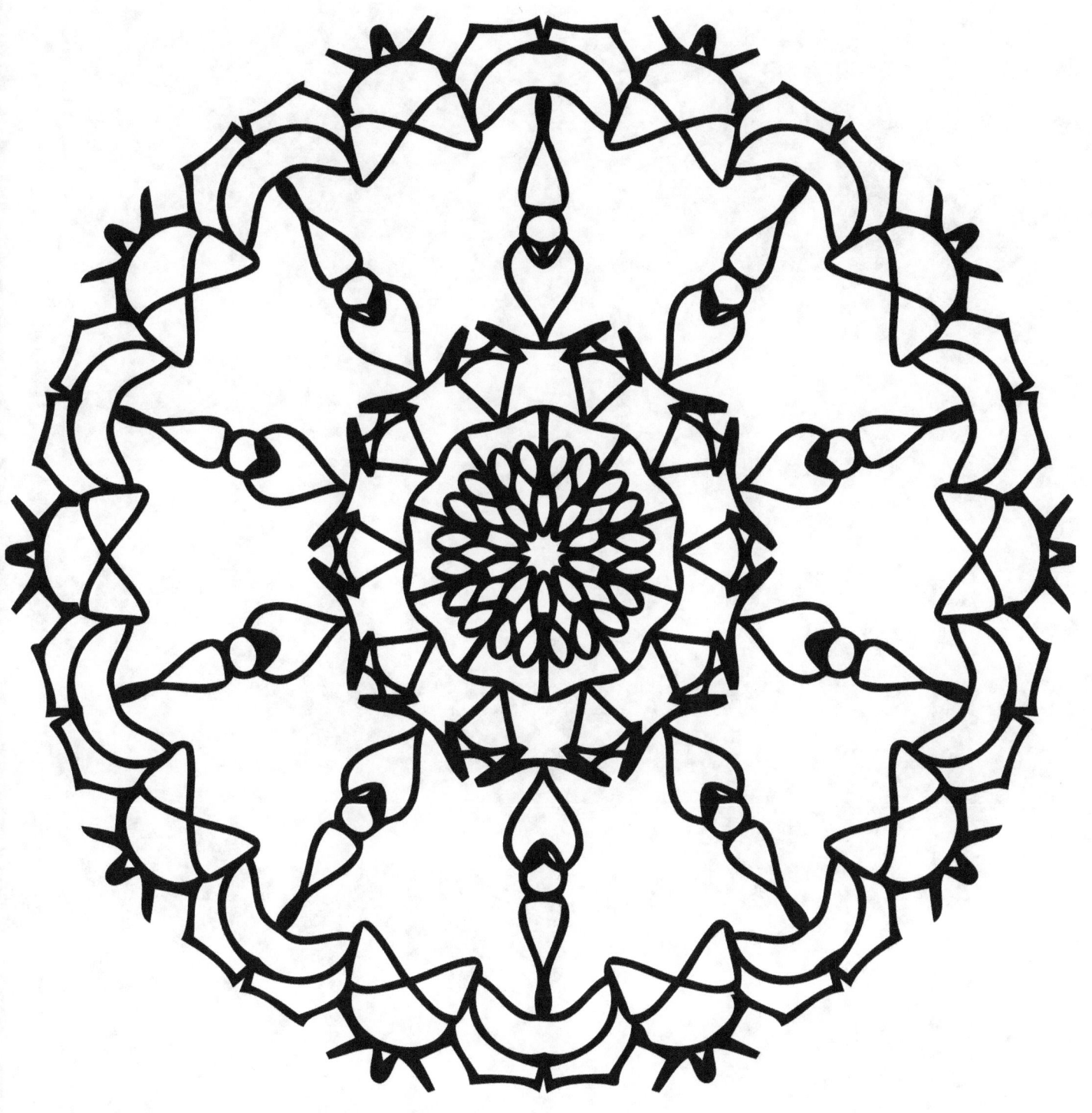

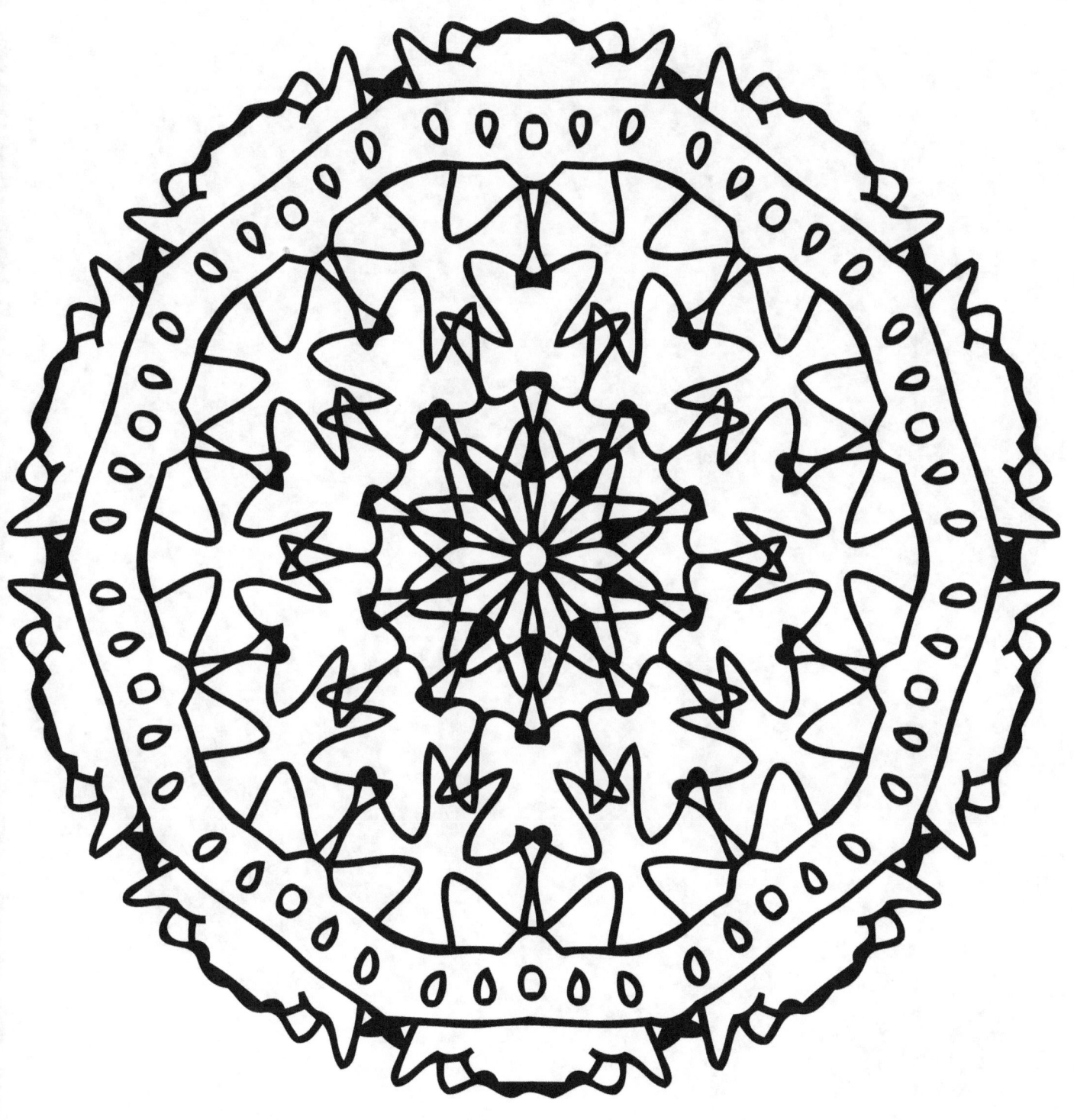

Illustrated by #cherylcolors
www.facebook.com/cherylcolors

Colored by: _____

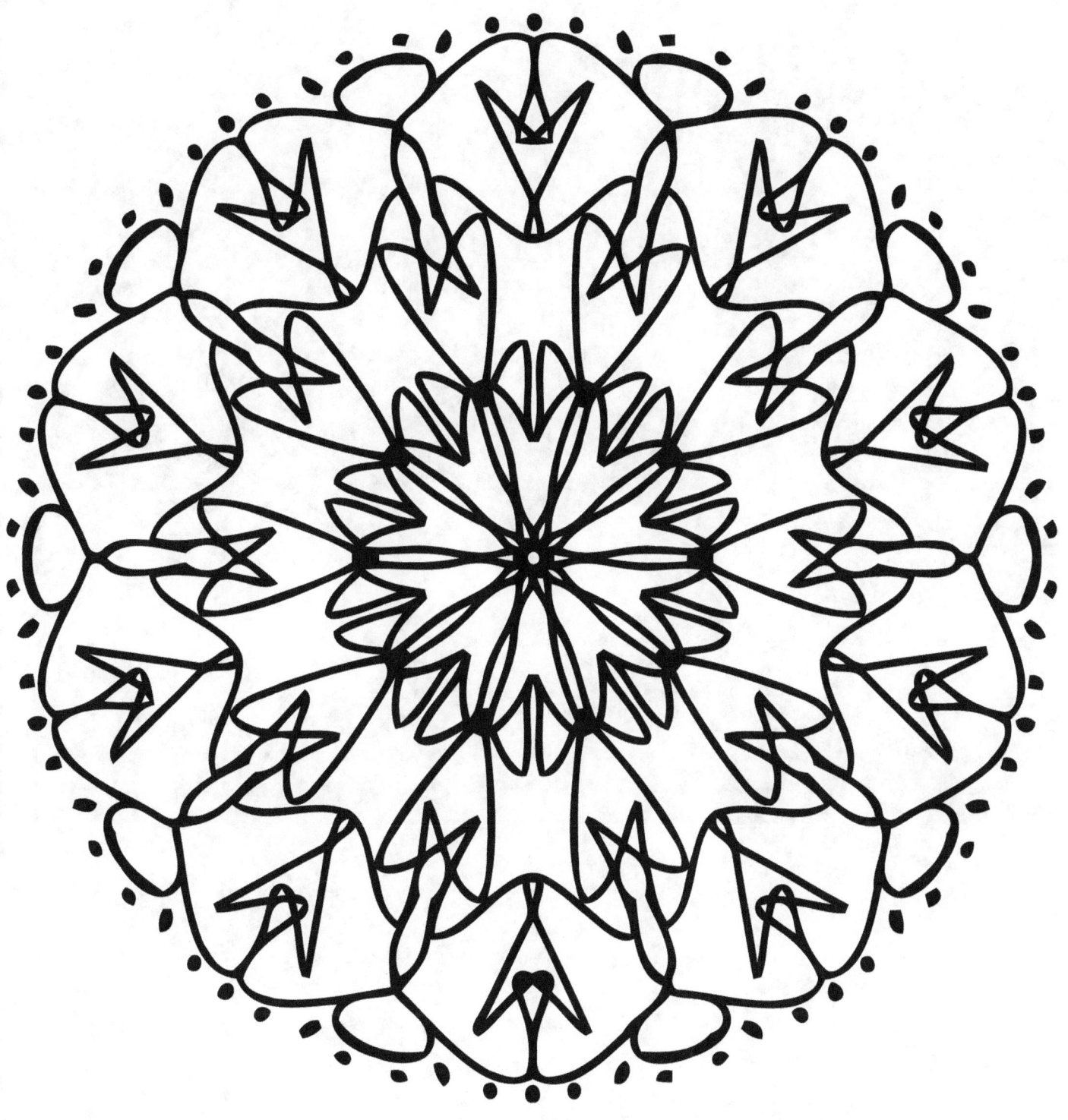

Illustrated by #cherylcolors
www.facebook.com/cherylcolors

Colored by: _____

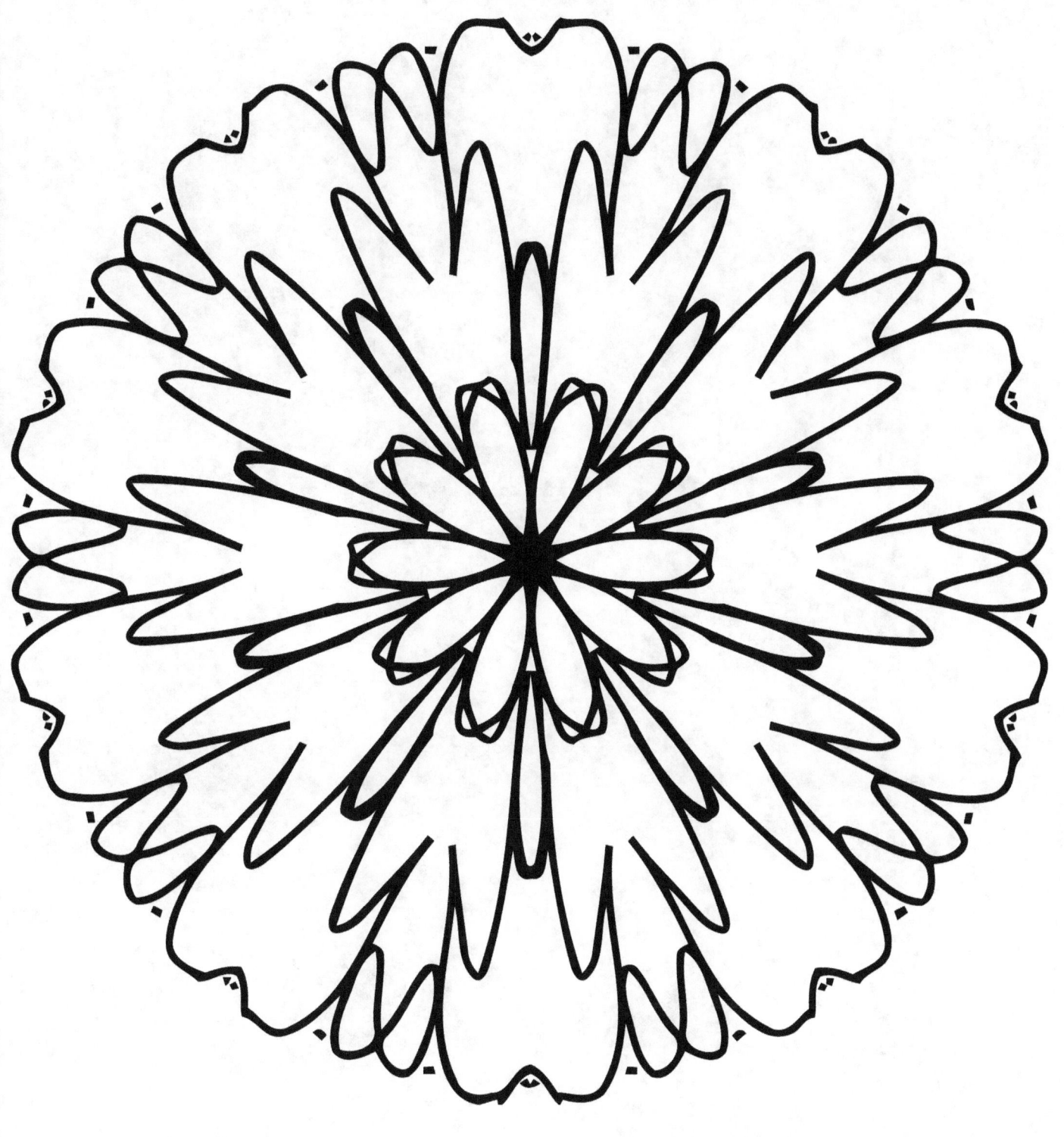

Illustrated by #cherylcolors
www.facebook.com/cherylcolors

Colored by: _____

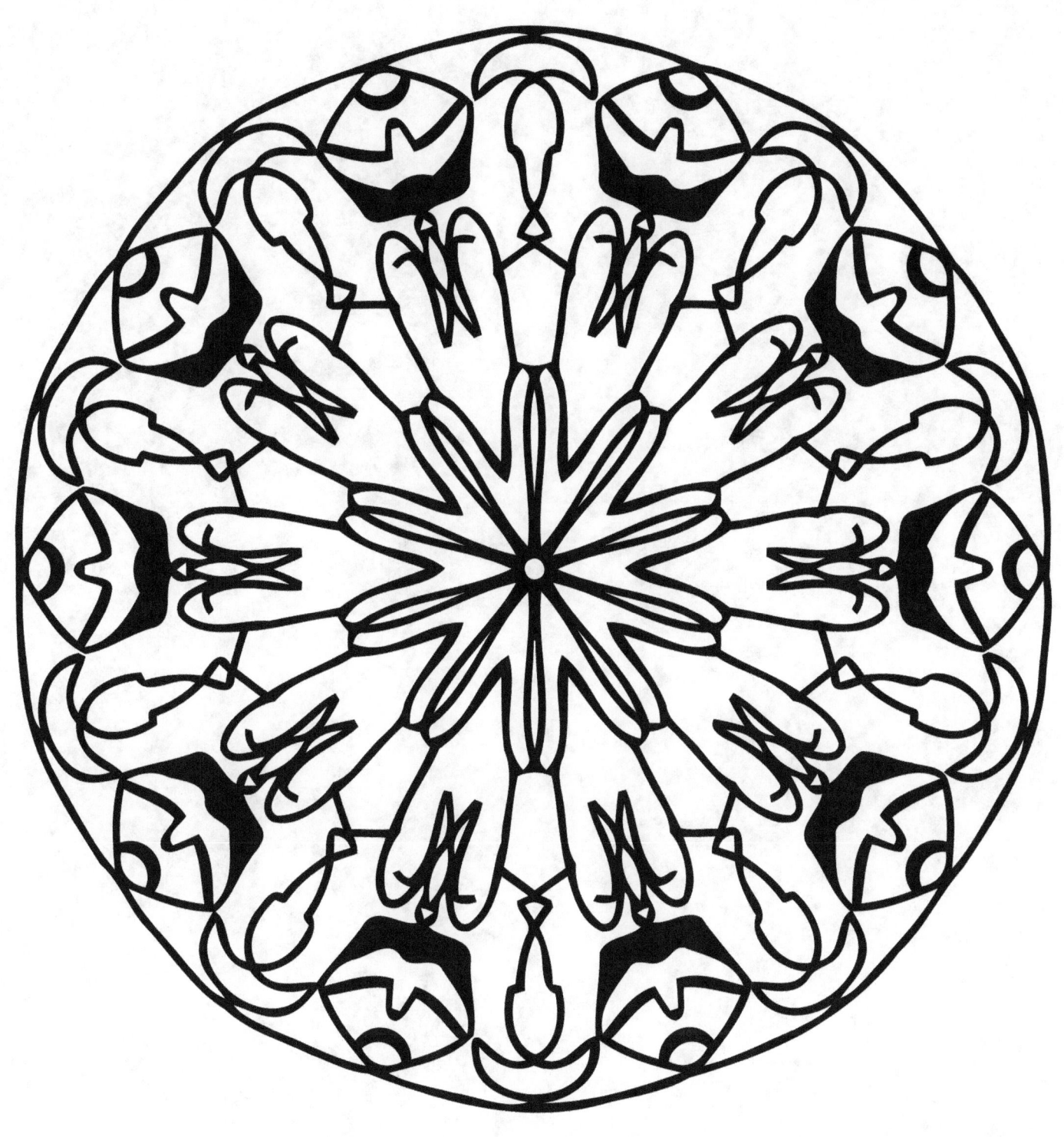

Illustrated by #cherylcolors
www.facebook.com/cherylcolors

Colored by: _____

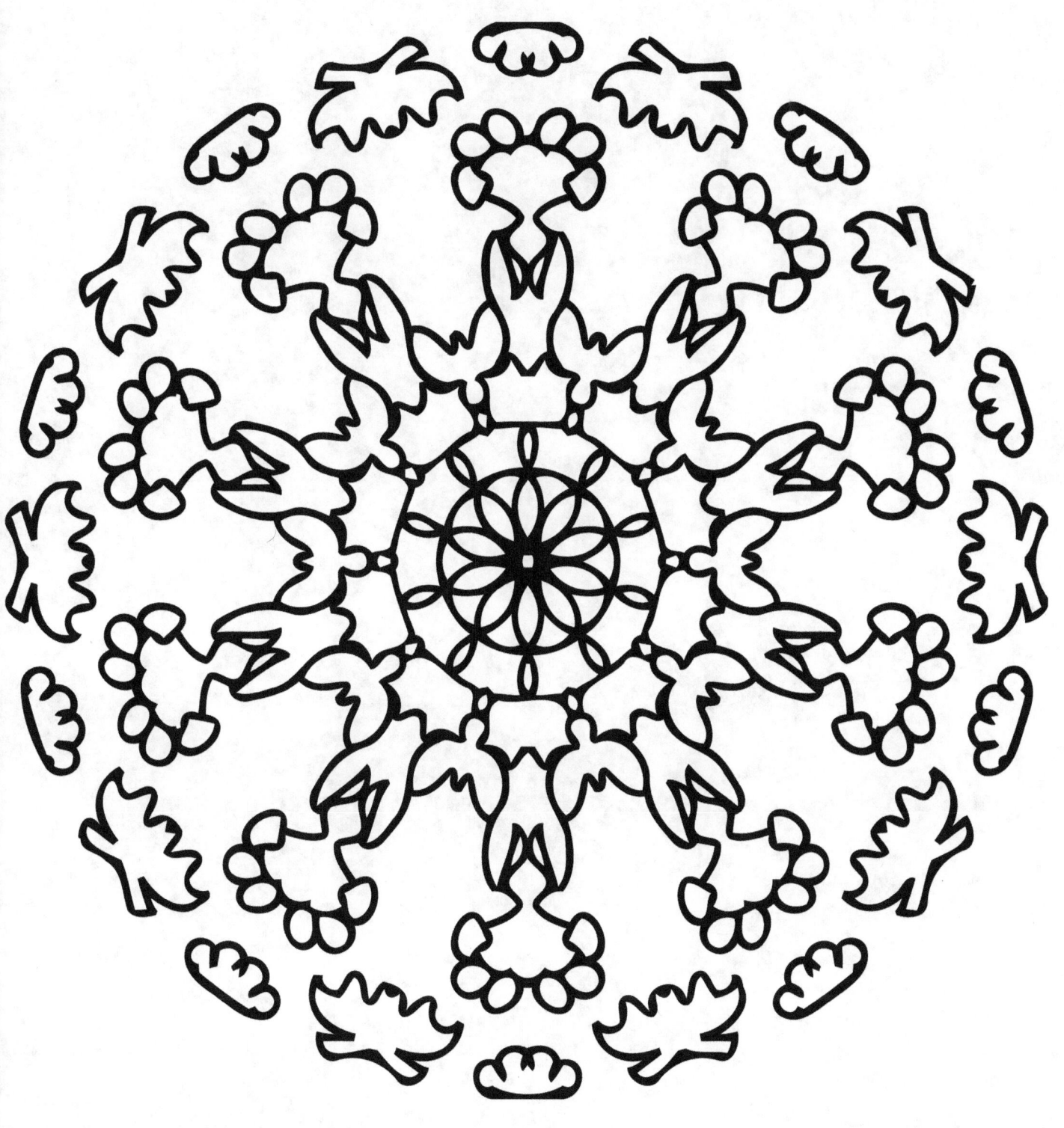

Illustrated by #cherylcolors
www.facebook.com/cherylcolors

Colored by: _____

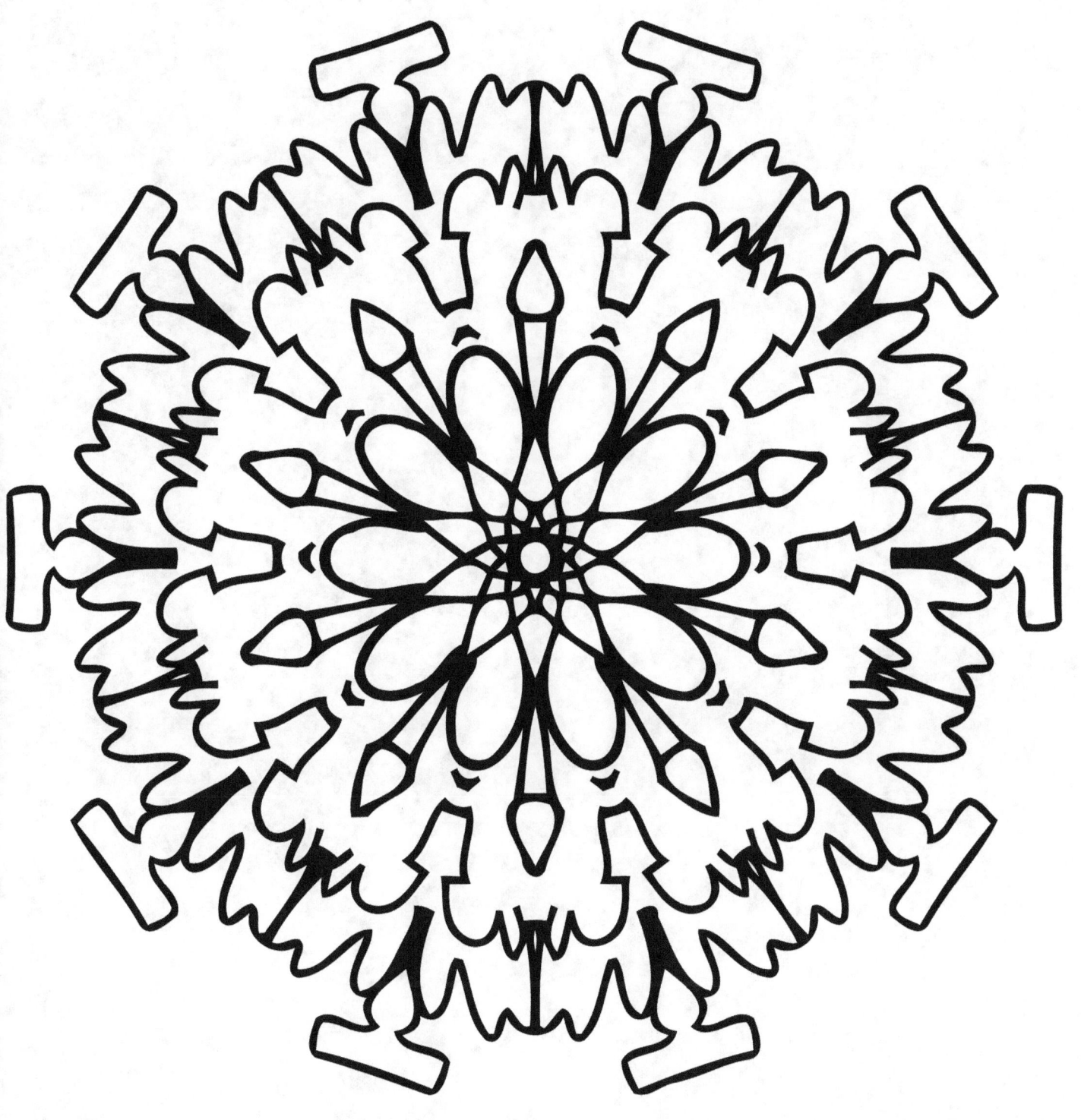

Illustrated by #cherylcolors
www.facebook.com/cherylcolors

Colored by: _____

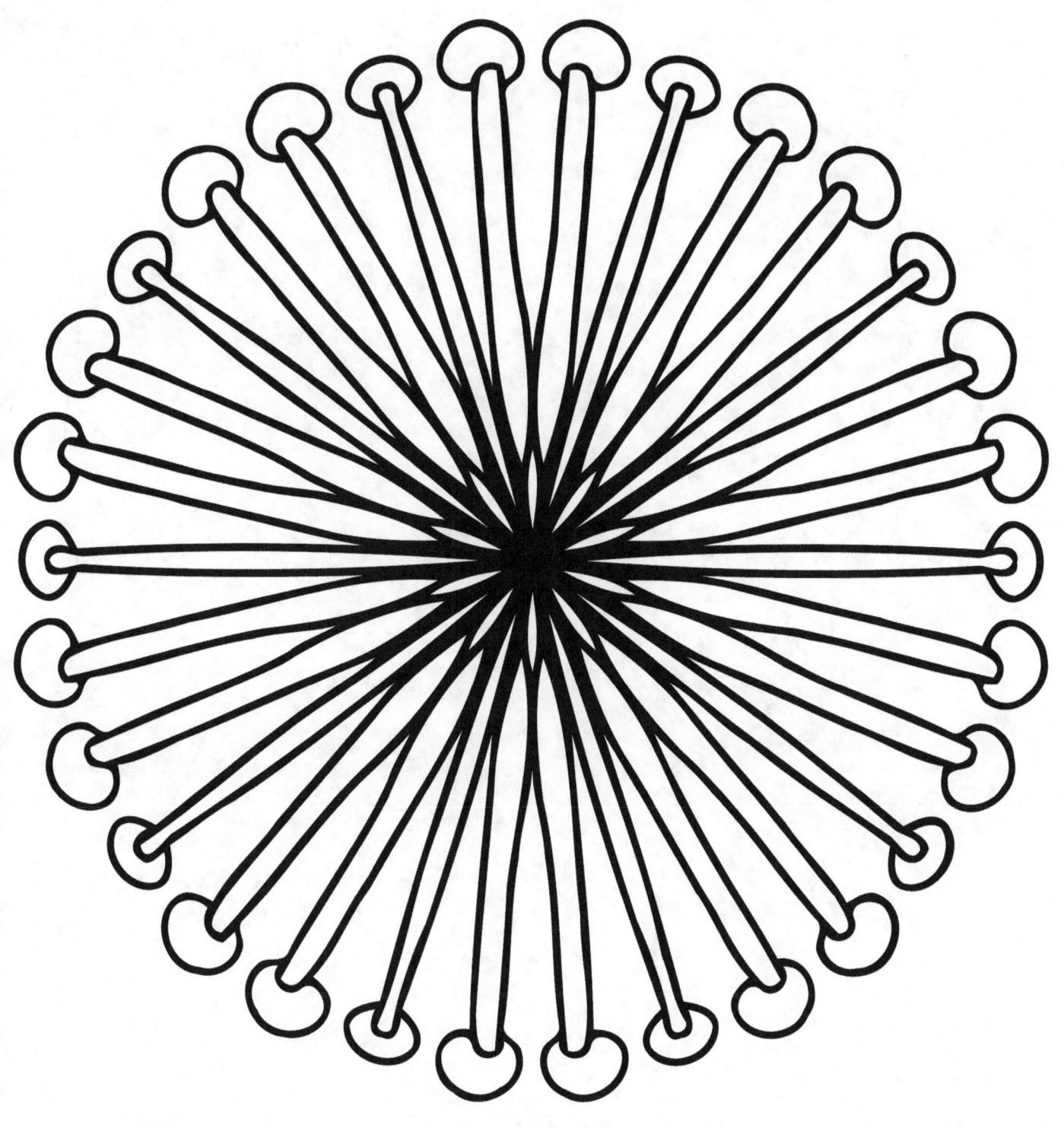

Illustrated by #cherylcolors
www.facebook.com/cherylcolors

Colored by: _____

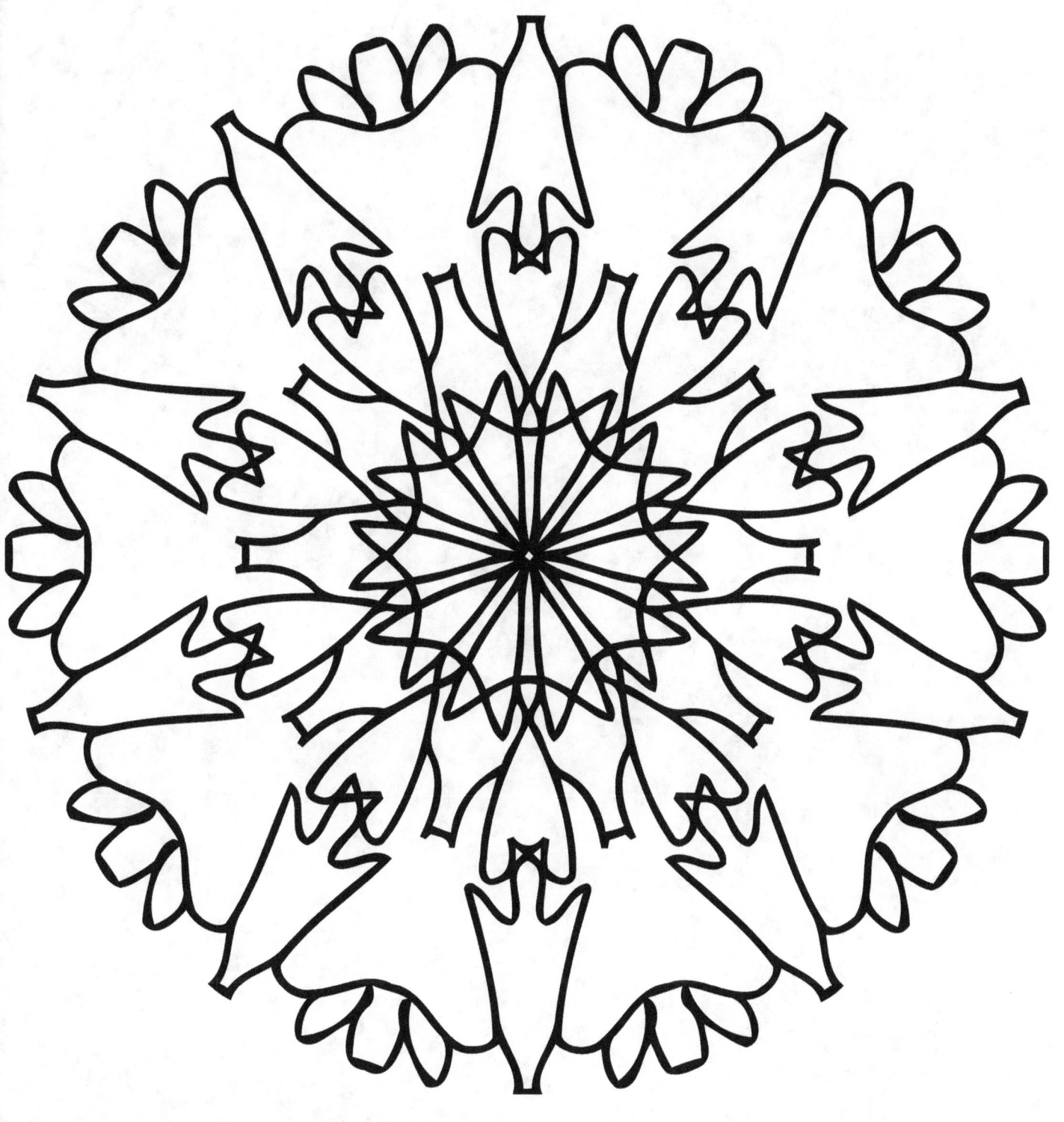

Illustrated by #cherylcolors
www.facebook.com/cherylcolors

Colored by: _____

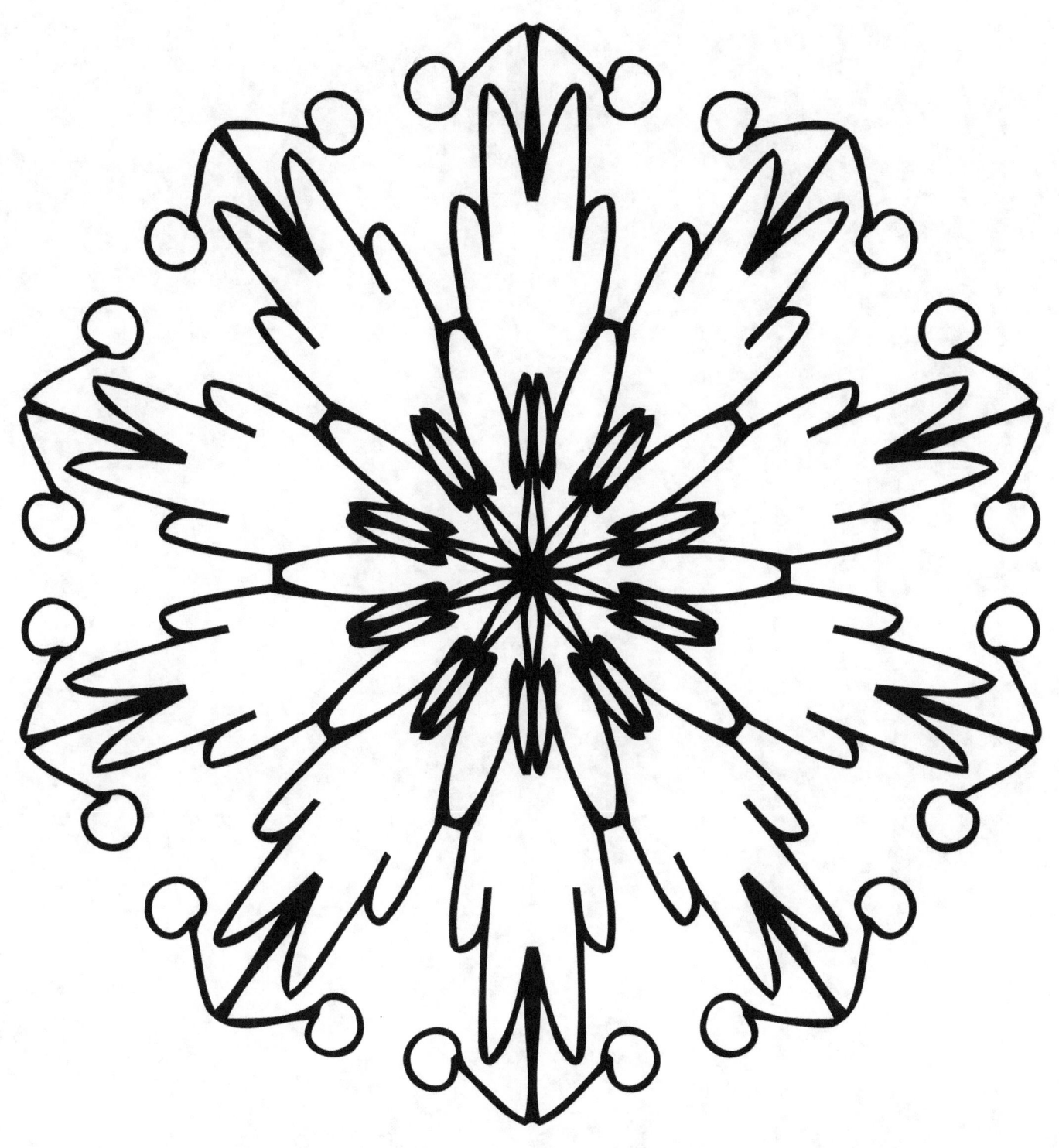

Illustrated by #cherylcolors
www.facebook.com/cherylcolors

Colored by: _____

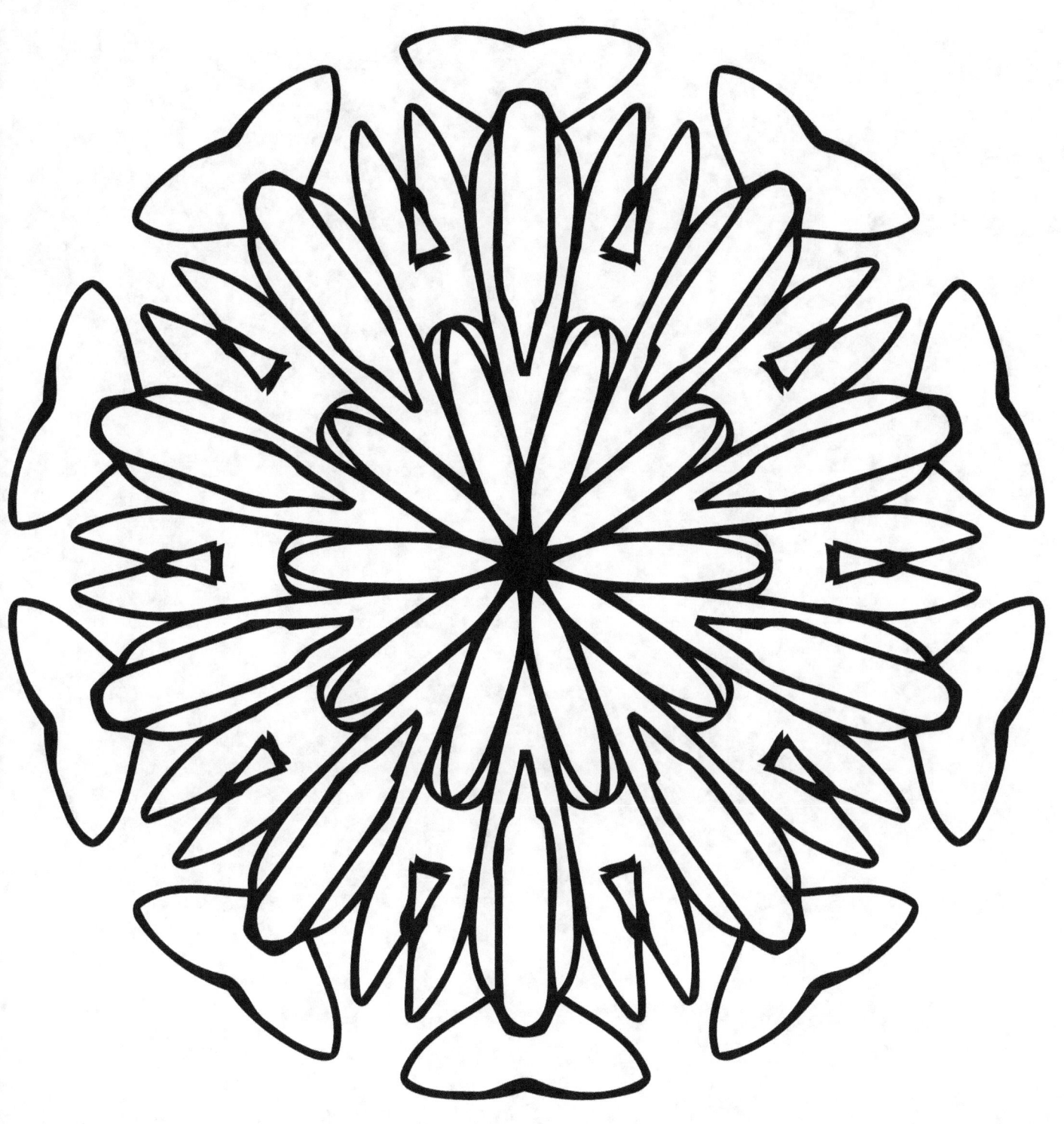

Illustrated by #cherylcolors
www.facebook.com/cherylcolors

Colored by: _____

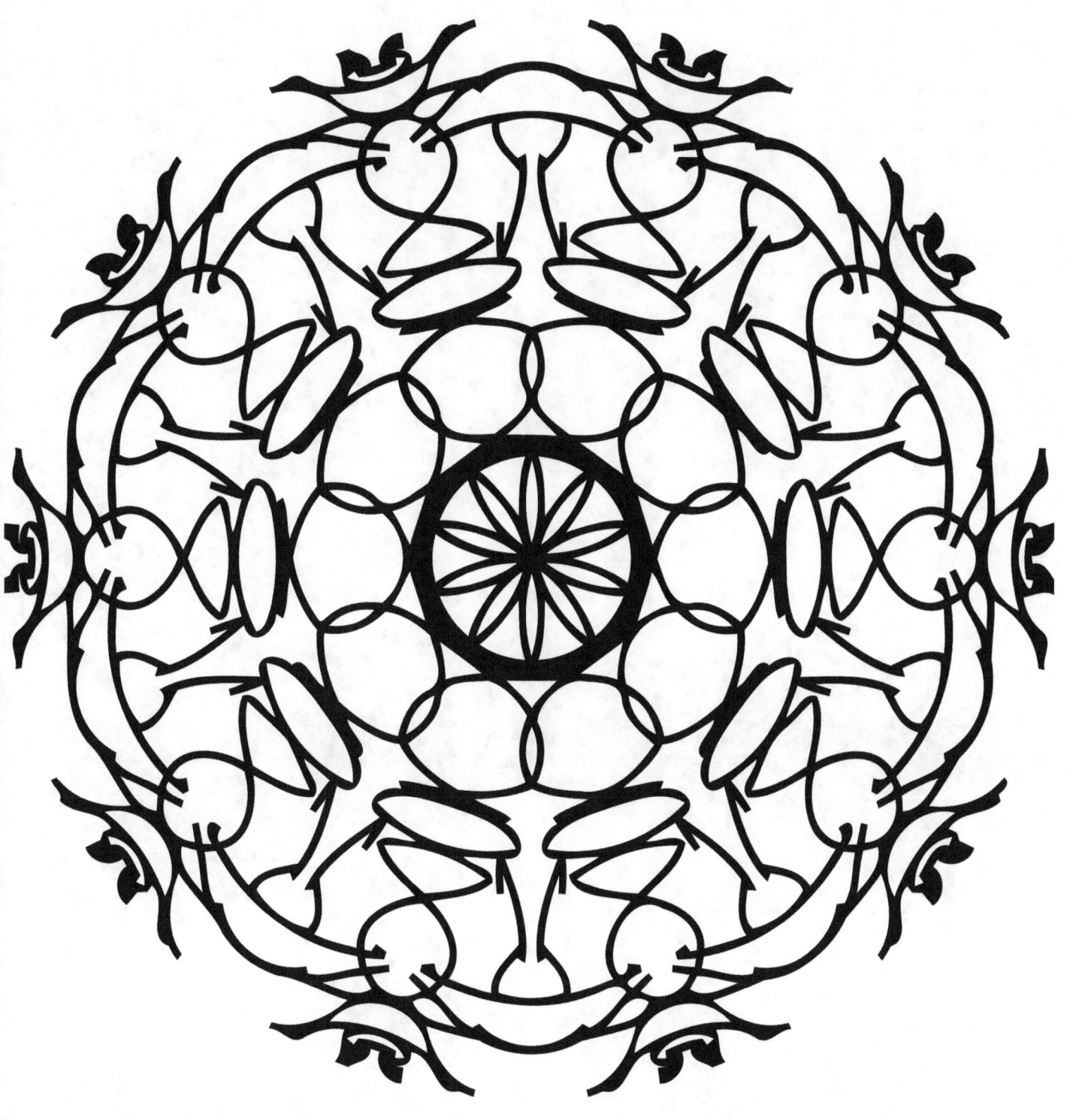

Illustrated by #cherylcolors
www.facebook.com/cherylcolors

Colored by: _____

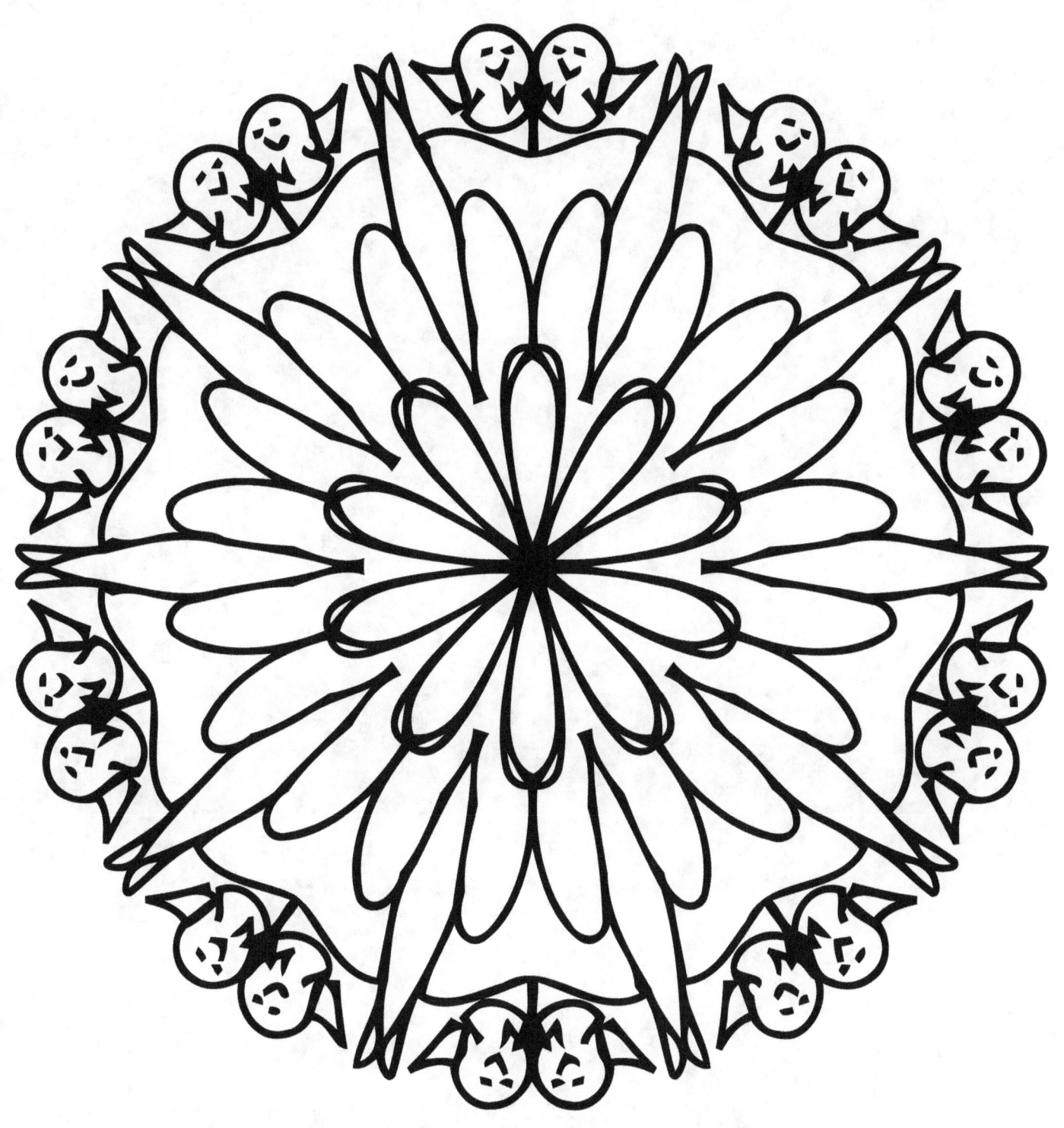

Illustrated by #cherylcolors
www.facebook.com/cherylcolors

Colored by: _____

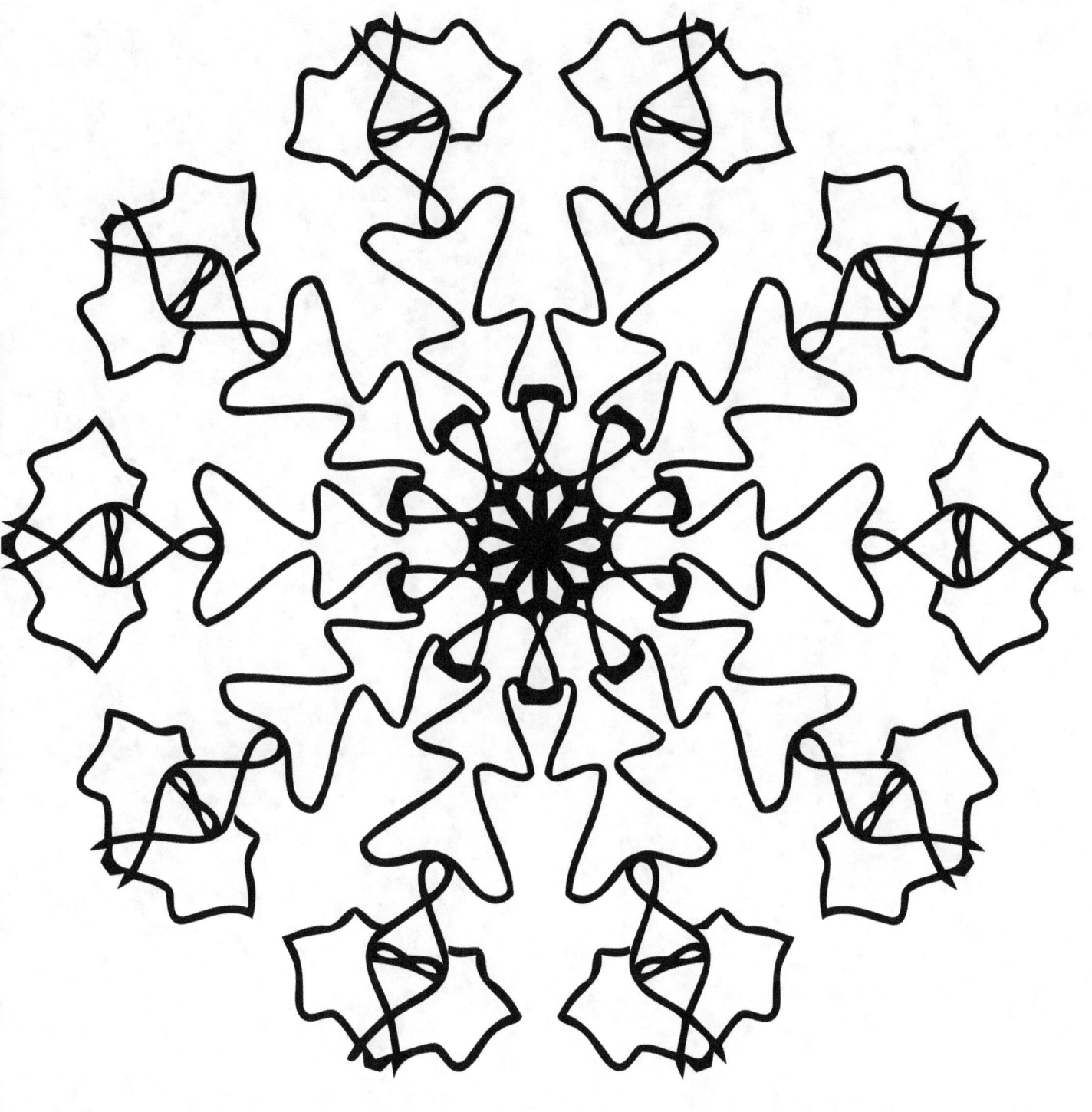

Illustrated by #cherylcolors
www.facebook.com/cherylcolors

Colored by: _____

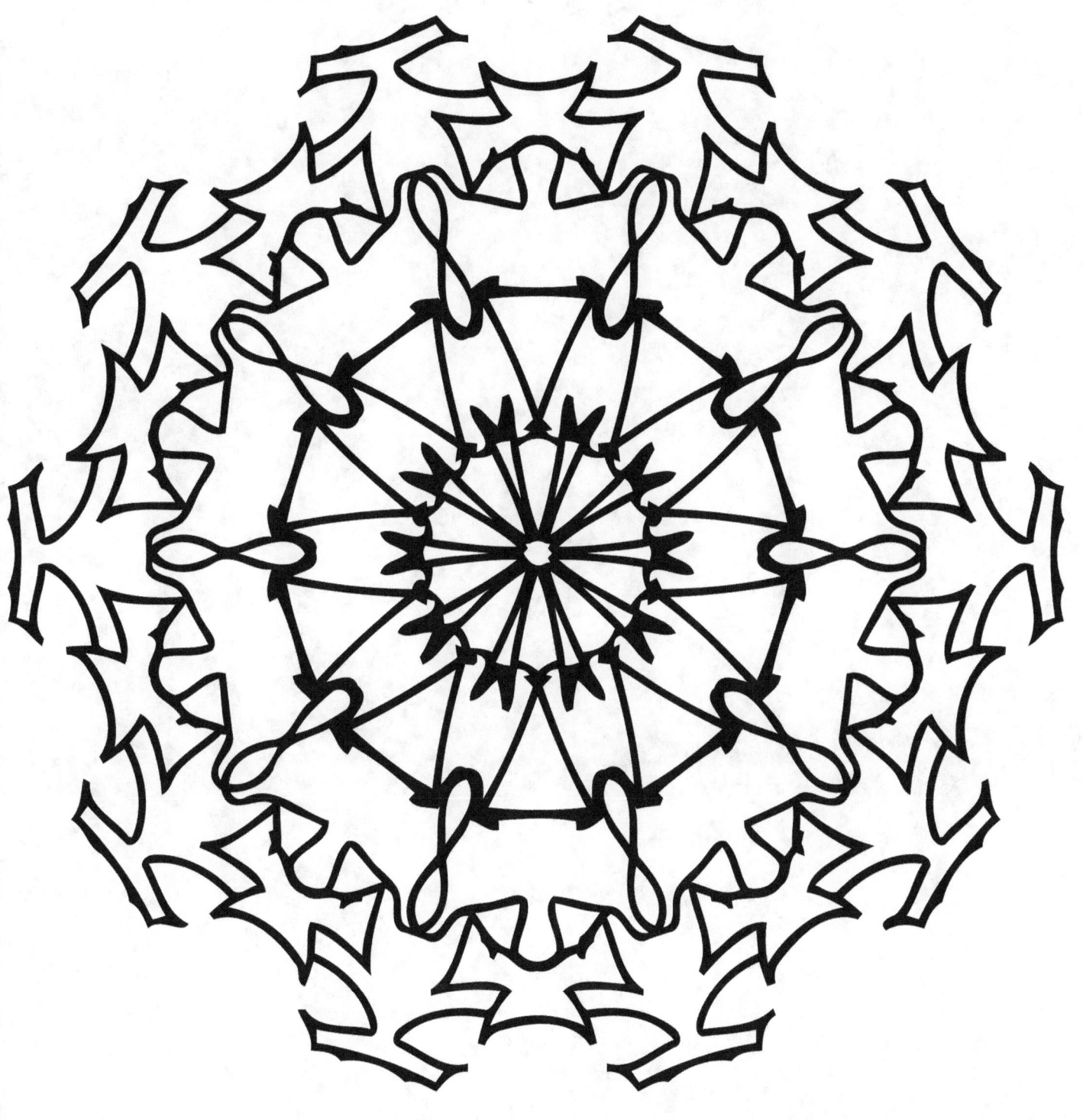

Illustrated by #cherylcolors
www.facebook.com/cherylcolors

Colored by: _____

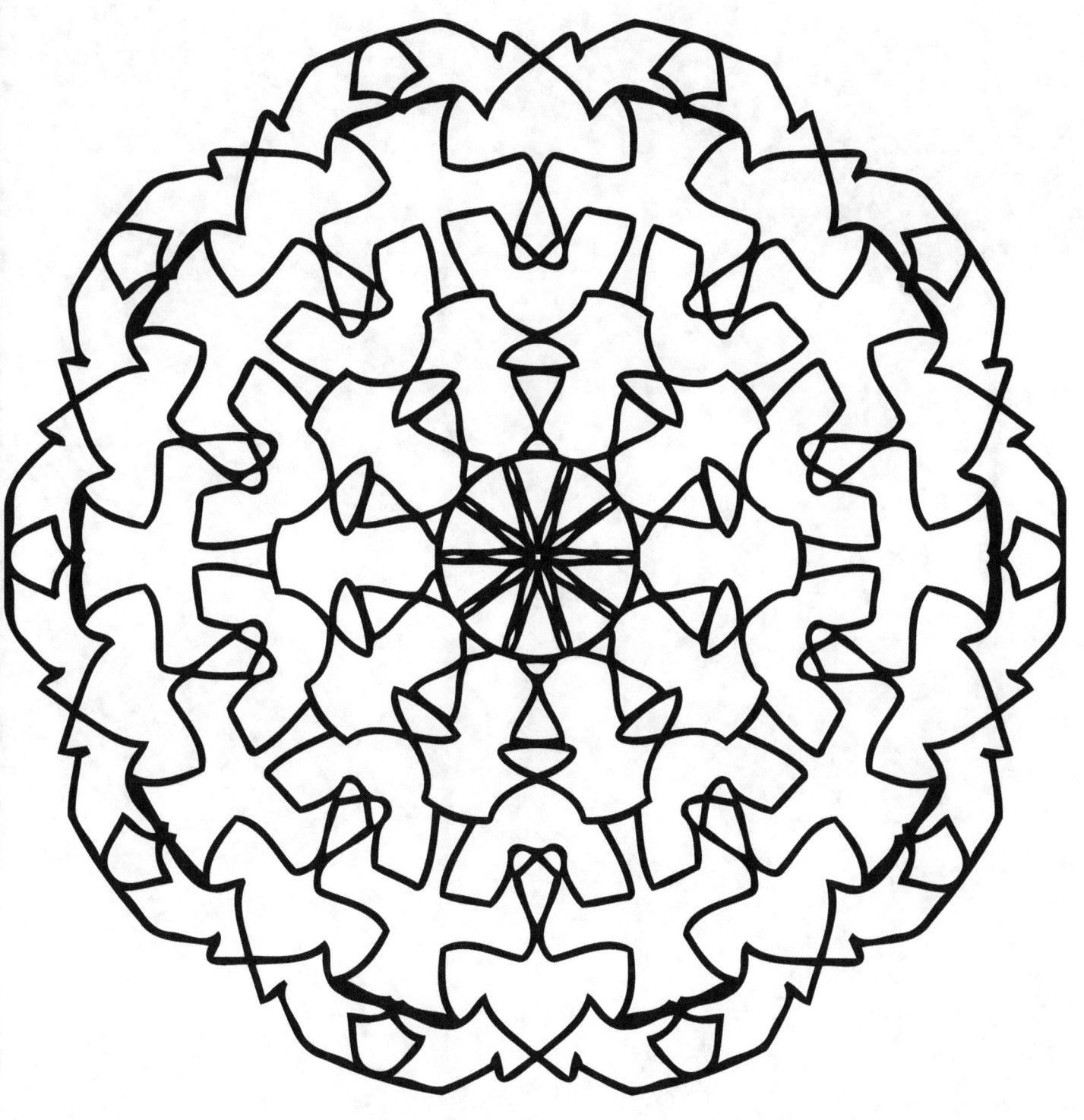

Illustrated by #cherylcolors
www.facebook.com/cherylcolors

Colored by: _____

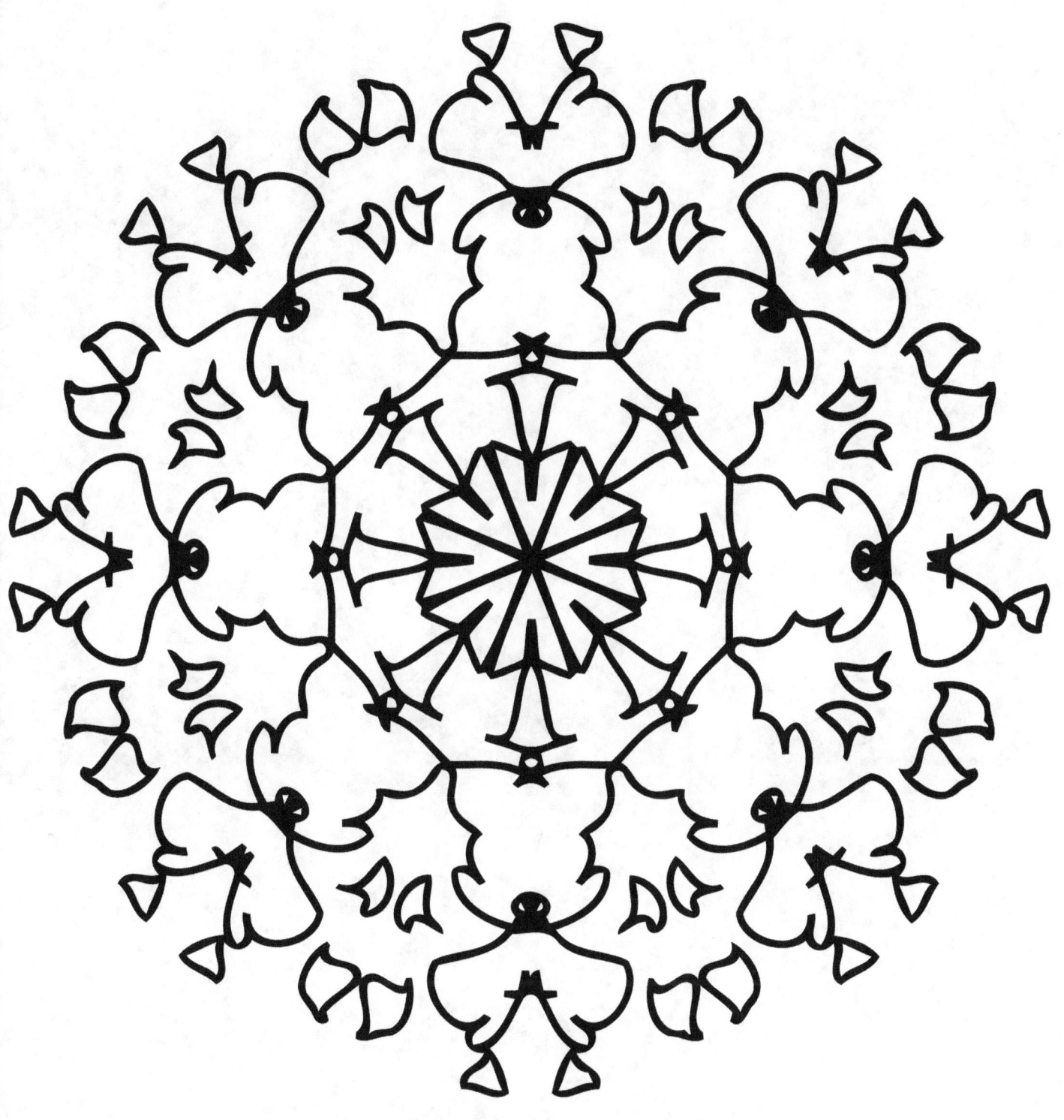

Illustrated by #cherylcolors
www.facebook.com/cherylcolors

Colored by: _____

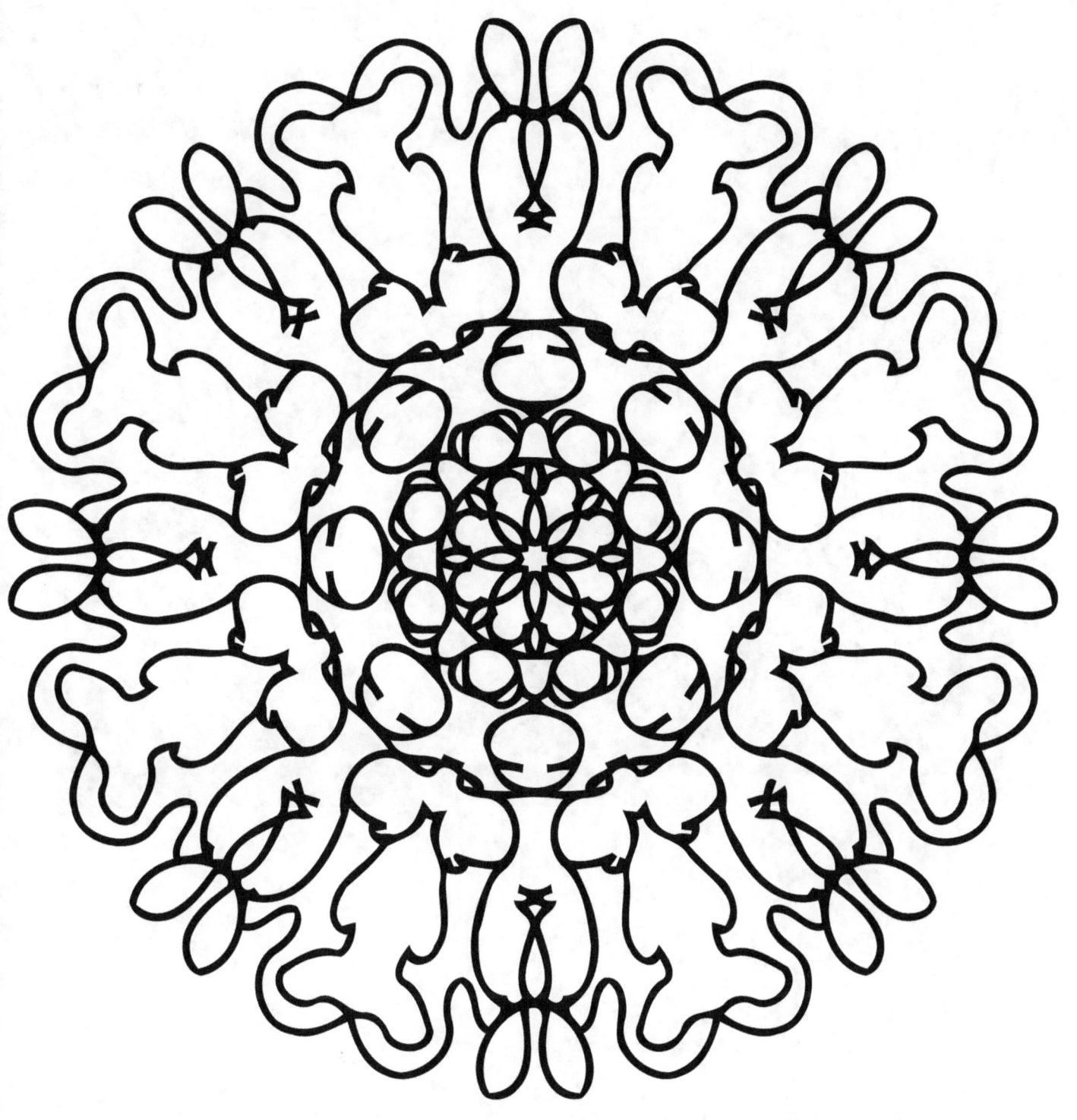

Illustrated by #cherylcolors
www.facebook.com/cherylcolors

Colored by: _____

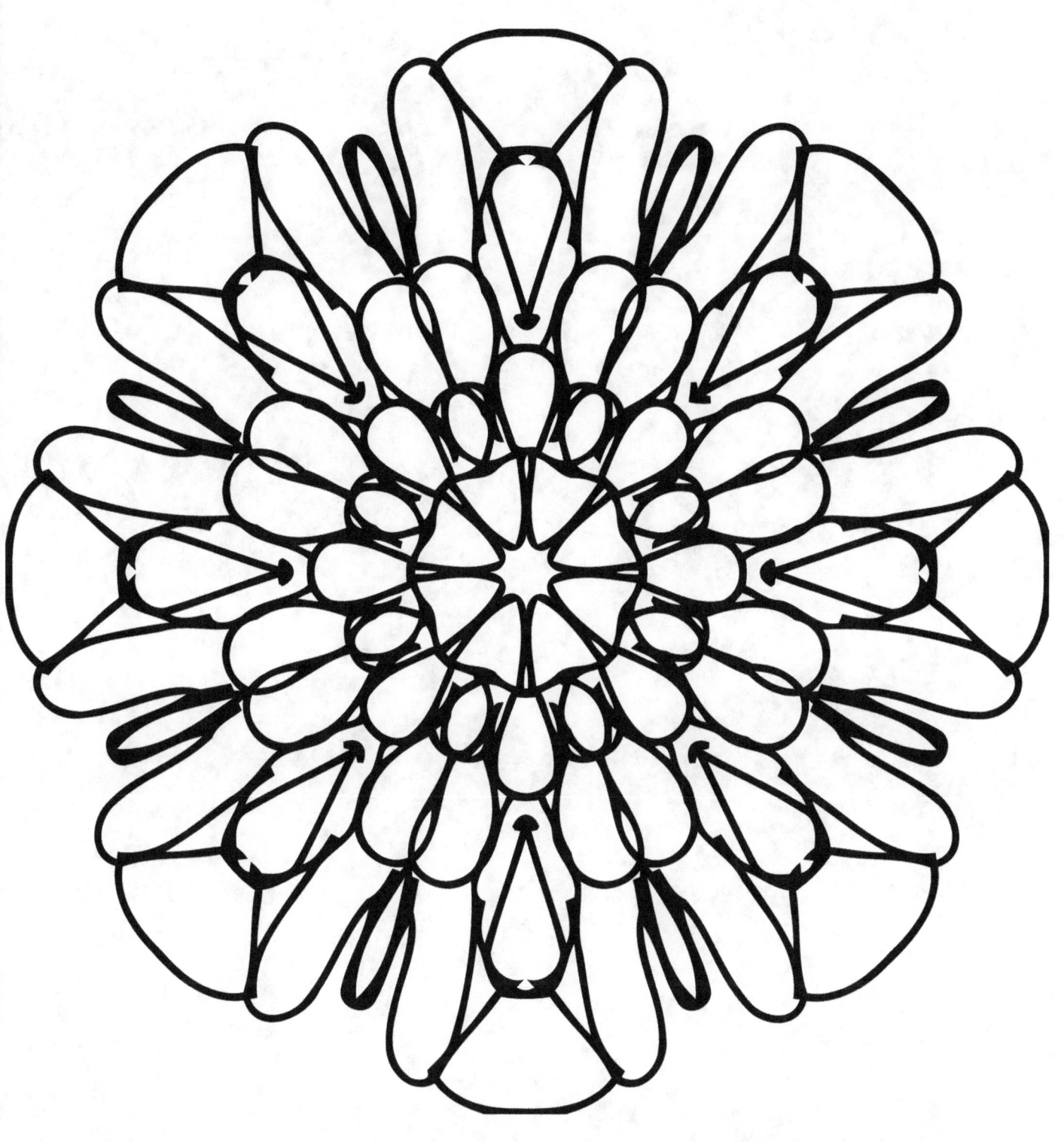

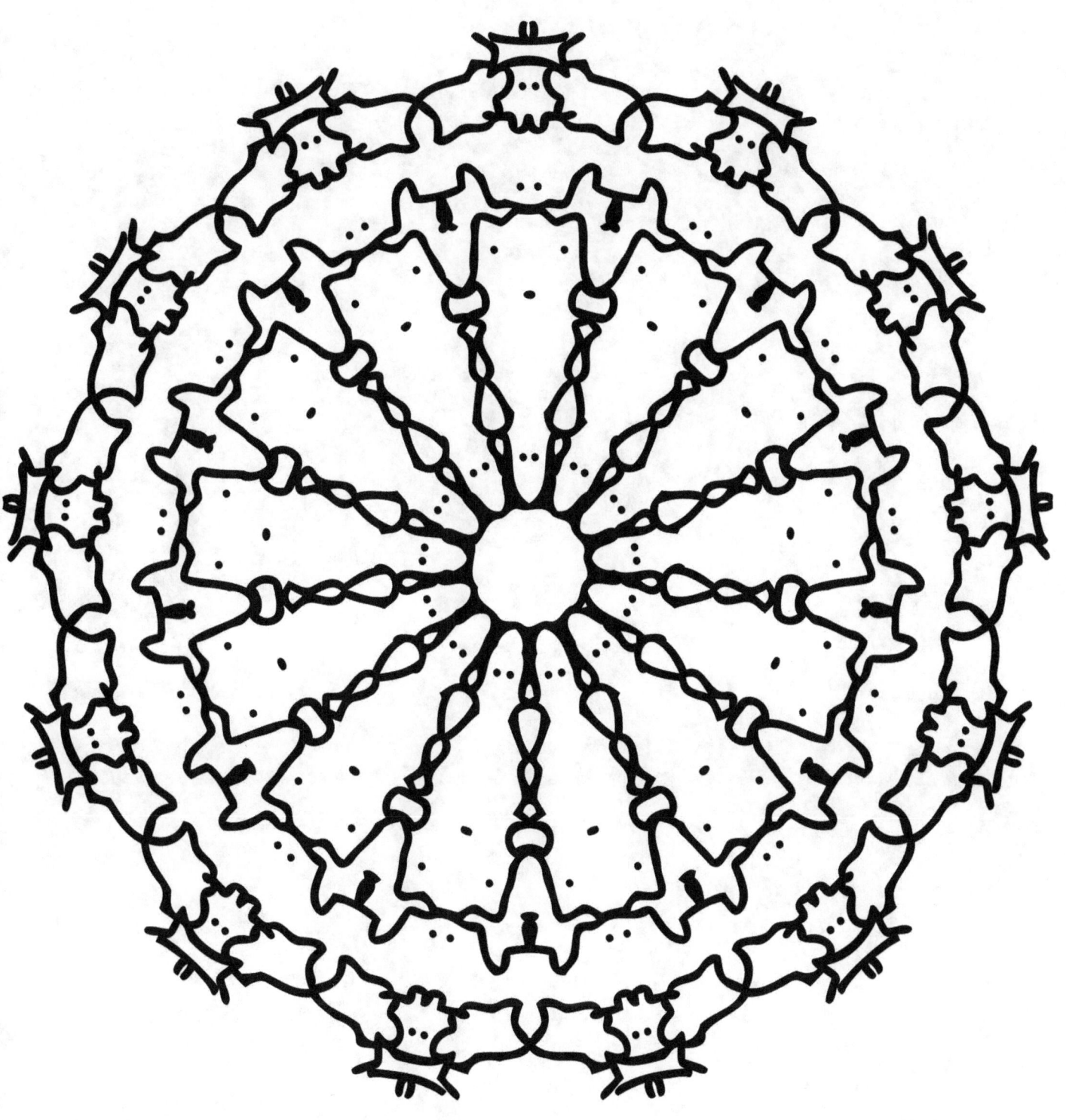

Illustrated by #cherylcolors
www.facebook.com/cherylcolors

Colored by: _____

The End

www.ingramcontent.com/pod-product-compliance
Lightning Source LLC
Chambersburg PA
CBHW082345220526
45470CB00008B/2652